The Autobiography of Mark Twain

By Mark Twain

The Illustrated Version

Picture of Mark Twain (Samuel Langhorne Clemens), taken in New York, in 1907; by photographer, A. F. Bradley.

From the Preface

In this Autobiography, I shall keep in mind the fact that I am speaking from the grave.... I shall be dead when the book issues from the press.... It seemed to me that I could be as frank and free as in a love letter if I knew that what I was writing would be exposed to no eye until I was dead, and unaware, and indifferent.

Mark Twain

CHAPTER 1

I WAS BORN THE 30TH OF NOVEMBER, 1835, in the almost invisible village of Florida, Missouri. My parents removed to Missouri in the early 'thirties; I do not remember just when, for I was not born then and cared nothing for such things. The village contained a hundred people and I increased the population by one percent. It is more than many of the best men in history could have done for a town. There is no record of a person doing as much — not even Shakespeare. But I did it for Florida.

Recently someone in Missouri has sent me a picture of the house I was born in. Heretofore I have always stated that it was a palace but I shall be more careful now.

Mark Twain's birthplace, Florida, Missouri.

The village has two streets, each a couple of hundred yards long, covered with stiff black mud in wet times, deep dust in dry. Most of the houses were of logs. There were none of brick and none of stone. There was a log church, which was a schoolhouse on week days. There were two stores in the village. My uncle owned one of them. It was very small, with a few rolls of cloth; a few barrels of salt fish, coffee, and sugar, brooms, axes, and other tools here and there; a lot of cheap hats and tin pans strung from the walls. At the other end of the room there were bags of shot, a cheese or two, and a barrel or so of whisky. If a boy bought five or ten cents' worth of anything he was entitled to a handful of sugar from the barrel; if a woman bought a few yards of cloth she was entitled to some thread; if a man bought something he was at liberty to swallow as big a drink of whisky as he wanted.

CHAPTER 2

My uncle was also a farmer, and his place was in the country four miles from Florida. I have not come across a better man than he was. I was his guest for two or three months every year, from the fourth year after we removed to Hannibal until I was eleven or twelve years old.

It was a heavenly place for a boy, that farm. The house was a double log one, with a spacious floor (roofed in) connecting it with the kitchen. In the summer the table was set in the middle of that shady and breezy floor, and the wonderful meals — well, it makes me cry to think of them.

The farmhouse stood in the middle of a very large yard and the yard was fenced on three sides; against these stood the smoke-house; beyond were the fruit trees and beyond them the Negro quarters and the tobacco fields. Down a way from the house stood a little log cabin against the fence, and there the woody hill fell sharply away to a brook which sang along over its stony bed and curved in and out and here and there in the deep shade of overhanging greenery — a divine place for going in barefoot, and it had swimming pools, too, which were forbidden to us and therefore much frequented by us. For we were little Christian children and had early been taught the value of forbidden fruit.

In the little log cabin lived a bedridden white-headed slave woman whom we visited daily and looked upon with wonder, for we believed she was upward of a thousand years old and had talked with Moses. We called her "Aunt" Hannah. Like the other Negroes, she was deeply religious.

All the Negroes were friends of ours. We had a faithful good friend in "Uncle Dan'l," a middle-aged slave whose head was the best one in the quarter, whose sympathies were wide and warm and whose heart was honest and simple. I have not seen him for more than half a century and yet spiritually I have had his welcome company a good part of that time. It was on the farm that I got my strong liking for his race and my appreciation of certain of its fine qualities. This feeling and this estimate have stood the test of sixty years and more.

CHAPTER 3

I CAN SEE THE FARM YET, WITH PERFECT CLEARNESS; I CAN SEE ALL ITS belongings, all its details; the family room of the house, the vast fireplace, piled high on winter nights with flaming logs; the lazy cat spread out in front of it; the sleepy dogs; my aunt in one chimney corner, knitting; my uncle in the other, smoking his pipe; the shiny and carpetless floor faintly mirroring the dancing flames; half a dozen children playing in the background.

Along outside of the front fence ran the country road, dusty in the summertime and a good place for snakes — they liked to lie in it and sun themselves. Beyond the road was a thick young woods and through it a dim-lighted path led a quarter of a mile. Down the forest slope to the left were the swings. They were made from young trees. When they became dry they were dangerous. They usually broke when a child was forty feet in the air and this was why so many bones had to be mended every year. I had no ill luck myself, but none of my cousins escaped. There were eight of them and at one time and another they broke fourteen arms among them. But it cost next to nothing, for the doctor worked by the year — twenty-five dollars for the whole family.

Doctors were not called in cases of ordinary illness; the family grandmother attended to those. Every old woman was a doctor and gathered her own medicines in the woods.

Doctor Meredith was our family physician and saved my life several times. Still, he was a good man and meant well. Let it go.

I was always told that I was a sickly and weak and tiresome and uncertain child and lived mainly on medicines during the first seven years of my life. I asked my mother about this, in her old age — she was in her eighty- eighth year — and said:

"I suppose that during all that time you were uneasy about me?"

"Yes, the whole time."

"Afraid I wouldn't live?"

After a thoughtful pause she said, "No — afraid you would."

CHAPTER 4

The country schoolhouse was three miles from my uncle's farm. It stood in a clearing in the woods, and would hold about twenty-five boys and girls. We attended the school with more or less regularity once or twice a week, in summer, walking to it in the cool of the morning by the forest paths and back in the growing dark. All the pupils brought their dinners in baskets and sat in the shade of the trees at noon and ate them. It is the part of my education which I look back upon with the most satisfaction.

As I have said, I spent some part of every year at the farm until I was twelve or thirteen years old. The life which I led there with my cousins was full of charm, and so is the memory of it yet. I can call back the mystery of the deep woods, the earthly smells, the faint odors of the wild flowers, the shining look of rainwashed leaves, the sound of drops when the wind shook the trees, the far-off noise of birds, the glimpses of disturbed wild creatures hurrying through the grass — I can call it all back and make it as real as it ever was, and as blessed. I can see the woods in their autumn dress of purple and gold and red, and I can hear the sound of the fallen leaves as we walked through them, and I can feel the pounding rain, upon my head, of the nuts as they fell when the wind blew them loose. I know the look of Uncle DanTs kitchen as it was at night, and I can see the white and black children with the firelight playing on their faces and the shadows dancing on the walls.

I can remember the bare wooden stairway in my uncle's house, and the turn to the left above the landing, and the sloping roof over my bed, and the squares of moonlight on the floor, and the white cold world of snow outside. I can remember the noise of the wind and the shaking of the house on stormy nights, and how warm and happy one felt, under the blankets, listening. I can remember how very dark that room was, in the dark of the moon — and on summer nights how pleasant it was to lie and listen to the rain on that roof, and enjoy the white glory of the lightning and the majestic crashing of the thunder. I remember the hunts for game and birds, and how we turned out, mornings, while it was still dark, and how chilly it was, and how often I regretted that I was well enough to go. Sounding a tin horn brought twice as many dogs as were needed, and in their happiness they raced about and knocked small people down and made no end of unnecessary noise. But presently the gray dawn stole over the world, the birds piped up, then the sun rose and poured light and comfort all around, everything was fresh and dewy and smelled good, and life was a joy again, and we would arrive back, tired, hungry, and just in time for breakfast.

CHAPTER 5

My father was John Marshall Clemens of Virginia; my mother Jane Lampton of Kentucky. My mother married my father in Lexington in 1823, when she was twenty years old and he twenty- four. Neither of them had very much in the way of property. She brought him two or three Negroes but nothing else, I think. They moved to the village of Jamestown, in the mountains. There their first children were born, but as I came at a much later time I do not remember anything about it. I was born in Missouri, an unknown new state and in need of attractions.

My father left a fine estate behind him in the region around Jamestown — 75,000 acres. When he died in 1847 he had owned it about twenty years. He had always said that the land would not become valuable in his time, but that it would be a good provision for his children some day. I wish I owned a couple of acres of that land right now, in which case I would not be writing autobiographies for a living. My mother's favorite cousin, James Lampton, always said of that land — and said it with blazing enthusiasm, too — "There's millions in it — millions." It is true that he always said that about everything — and was always mistaken, too, but this time he was right; which shows that if a man will keep up his heart and fire at everything he sees he will surely hit something.

James Lampton floated, all his days, in a world of dreams and died at last without seeing a one of them realized. He was, when I saw him last in 1884, old and white-haired but he entertained me in the same old way of his earlier life and he still had a happy light in his eye and hope in his heart — and he could still share the secret riches of the world with me.

CHAPTER 6

My father bought the enormous area of around 100,000 acres at one purchase. The entire lot must have cost him somewhere in the neighborhood of four hundred dollars. That was a good deal of money to pass over at one payment in those days. When my father paid down that great sum and turned and stood in the courthouse door of Jamestown and looked abroad over his vast possessions, he said, "Whatever happens to me, my children will be secure; I shall not live to see these acres turn to silver and gold but my children will." Thus with the very kindest intentions in the world toward us he laid the heavy curse of future wealth upon our shoulders. He went to his grave in the full belief that he had done us a kindness. It was a sorrowful mistake but fortunately he never knew it.

My eldest brother was four or five years old when the great purchase was made, and my eldest sister was a child in arms. The rest of us came afterwards, and were born along from time to time during the next ten years. Four years after the purchase came the great financial crash of 1834 and in that storm my father's fortunes were wrecked. From being honored and envied as the richest citizen of the county he suddenly woke up and found himself reduced to almost nothing. He was a proud man, a silent man, and not a person to live among the scenes of his vanished grandness and be the subject for public pity. He gathered together his household and journeyed many weary miles toward what then was the "Far West," and at last came to the little town of Florida, Missouri. He ran a store there several years but had no luck, except that I was born to him. He presently removed to Hannibal and rose there to be an officer of the court when the summons came that no man can disregard.

But even upon his deathbed he thought of his land. He said that it would make us all rich and happy. And so believing, he died.

We turned our waiting eyes upon this land, and through all our wanderings and all our good times and bad over continents and seas between, we were possessed with an old habit and a faith that rises and falls but never dies. We were always going to be rich next year — so why work? It is good to begin life poor; it is good to begin life rich — these are wholesome; but to begin it poor but prospectively rich! The man who has not experienced it cannot imagine the curse of it.

CHAPTER 7

When my mother died in October 1890 she was in her eighty- eighth year, a mighty age, a well-fought fight for life for one who at forty was so delicate of body as to be considered an invalid and soon to die. I knew her well during the first twenty-five years of my life; but after that I saw her only at wide intervals, for we lived many days' journey apart. I am not proposing to write about her but merely to talk about her.

What becomes of the many photographs which one's mind takes of people? Out of the millions of this, my first and closest friend, only one clear one of early date remains. It goes back forty-seven years; she was forty years old then, and I was eight. She held me by the hand and we were on our knees by the bedside of my brother, two years older than I, who lay dead, and the tears were flowing down her cheeks.

She had a slender, small body but a large heart — a heart so large that everybody's grief and everybody's joys found welcome in it. The greatest difference which I find between her and the rest of the people whom I have known is this: those others felt a strong interest in a few things, but to the very day of her death she felt a strong interest in the whole world and everything and everybody in it. In all her life she never knew such a thing as a halfhearted interest in affairs and people, or an interest which drew a line and left out certain affairs and was indifferent to certain people.

Her interest in people and other animals was warm, personal, friendly. She always found something to excuse, and as a rule to love, in the roughest of them — even if she had to put it there herself. She was the natural friend of the friendless.

One day in St. Louis she walked out into the street and greatly surprised a cartman who was beating his horse over the head with a handle of his heavy whip; for she took the whip away from him and forced him to promise that he would never be cruel to a horse again. That sort of action in the cause of mistreated animals was a common thing with her all her life, and her manner and intent always carried her point and sometimes won the friendship of the very people she challenged. The homeless, hunted, and meanest of cats followed her home, and were welcome. We had nineteen cats at one time, in 1845. And there wasn't one in the lot that had any character, not one that had any merit. They were a vast burden to all of us — including my mother — but they were out of luck and that was enough; they had to stay. However, better these than no pets at all; children must have pets and we were not allowed to have caged ones. My mother would not have allowed a rat to be imprisoned.

CHAPTER 8

My school days began when I WAS four years and a half old. There were no public schools in Missouri in those early years but there were two private schools — at twenty-five cents per week and collect it if you can. Mrs. Horr taught the children in a small log house at the southern end of Main Street. Mr. Sam taught the young people of larger growth in a frame schoolhouse on the hill. I was sent to Mrs. Horr's school and I remember my first day in that little log house with perfect clearness, after these sixty-five years and upwards.

Mrs. Horr was a New England lady of middle age with New Eng- land ways and principles and she always opened school with prayer and a chapter from the New Testament; also she explained the chapter with a brief talk. In one of these talks she spoke about "Ask and ye shall receive," and said that whoever prayed for a thing with earnestness and strong desire need not doubt that his prayer would be answered.

I was so forcibly struck with this information and so pleased by the opportunities that it offered that I thought I would give it a trial. I prayed for gingerbread. Margaret Kooneman, who was the baker's daughter, brought a piece of gingerbread to school every morning; she had always kept it out of sight before but when I finished my prayer and glanced up, there it was in easy reach and she was looking the other way. In all my life I never enjoyed an answer to prayer more than that one; and I was convinced, too. I had no end of wants and they had always remained unsatisfied up to that time, but I meant to supply them and increase them now that I had found out how to do it.

But this dream was like almost all the other dreams we have in life: there was nothing to it. I did as much praying during the next two or three days as anyone in that town, I suppose, and I was very honest and earnest about it too, but nothing came of it. I found that not even the most powerful prayer could lift that gingerbread again, and I came to the conclusion that if a person remains faithful to his gingerbread and keeps his eye on it he need not trouble himself about prayers.

Something about the way I was acting troubled my mother and she took me aside and questioned me. I did not want to reveal to her the change that had come over me, for it would grieve me to distress her kind heart, but at last I confessed, with many tears, that I had ceased being a Christian. She was heartbroken and asked me why.

I said it was because I had found out that I was a Christian just for what I could get out of it, and I could not bear the thought of that.

She gathered me to her breast and comforted me. I had gathered from what she said that if I would continue in that condition I would never be lonely.

My mother had a good deal of trouble with me but I think she enjoyed it. She had none at all with my brother Henry, who was two years younger than I, and I think that all his goodness and truthfulness, obeying everybody, would have been a burden to her but for the relief which I furnished in the other direction. I was valuable to her. I never thought of it before but now I see it.

CHAPTER 9

In 1849, WHEN I WAS fourteen years old, we were still living in Hannibal, on the banks of the Mississippi, in the new frame house built by my father five years before. That is, some of us lived in the new part, the rest in the old part back of it and attached to it.

66 year old Mark Twain revisiting his old home, in Hannibal, Missouri, in 1902.

In the autumn my sister gave a party and invited all the marriage-able people of the village. I was too young for this society and too retiring to mix with young ladies, anyway, therefore I was not invited — at least not for the whole evening. Ten minutes of it was to be my whole share. I was to do the part of a bear in a small fairy play. I was to wear a close-fitting suit of brown hairy stuff suitable for a bear.

About half past ten I was told to go to my room and put on this suit. I started but changed my mind, for I wanted to practice a little and the room was very small. I crossed over to a large unoccupied house on the corner of Main Street, not knowing that a dozen of the young people were also going there to dress for their parts.

I took my friend Sandy with me and we selected a large, roomy and empty chamber on the second floor. We entered it talking, and that gave a couple of half- dressed ladies an opportunity to hide behind a screen. Their gowns and things were hanging on hooks behind the door but I did not see them.

There was an old screen across the room, with many holes in it, but as I did not know there were girls behind it I was not disturbed by that detail. If I had known, I could not have undressed in the flood of cruel moonlight that was pouring in at the curtainless windows; I should have died of shame. Untroubled by this, I was naked to the skin and I began my practice. I was full of ambition. I was determined to succeed. I was burning to establish a reputation as a bear and get further engagements; so I threw myself into my work with an abandon that promised great things. I went back and forth from one room to the other on all fours, Sandy cheering; I walked upright and made the noises I thought a bear should make. I stood on my head; I danced from side to side; I did everything a bear could do and many things which no bear could ever do and no bear with any dignity would want to do, anyway, and of course I never suspected that I was making a spectacle of myself to anyone but Sandy. At last, standing on my head, I paused in that attitude to take a minute's rest.

All of a sudden there was a burst of girlish laughter from behind the screen. All the strength went out of me and brought the screen right down with my weight, burying the young ladies under it. In their fright they discharged a couple of loud screams. I picked up my clothes and ran, Sandy following. I was dressed in half a minute and out the back way. I made Sandy promise to be silent and then we went and hid until the party was over.

The house was very still and everybody asleep when I finally dared go home. I was very heavy-hearted and full of a bitter sense of my crime. Pinned to my pillow I found a slip of paper which bore a line which read: "You probably couldn't have played bear but you played bare very well — oh, very very well!" [Editor's note: bare, meaning naked, and bear, meaning the animal, are pronounced so that they sound the same, and this is a play on words.]

But a boy's life is not all fun; much of the tragic enters into it. The drunken wanderer who was burned up in the village prison lay upon my conscience a hundred nights afterward and filled them with ugly dreams — dreams in which I saw his appealing face as I had seen it in the sad reality, pressed against the window bars, with the red hell glowing behind him — a face which seemed to say to me, "If you had not given me the matches this would not have happened; you are responsible for my death." I was not responsible, for I had meant him no harm but only good when I let him have the matches. The tramp — who was guilty — suffered ten minutes; I, who was not to blame, suffered three months.

All within the space of a couple of years we had two or three other tragedies and I had the ill luck to be too nearby on each occasion. My teaching and training enabled me to see deeper into these tragedies than an uneducated person could have done. But as a rule they could not stand the daylight. They faded out and disappeared in the glad sunshine. They were the creatures of fear and darkness. The day gave me cheer and peace and at night I was sorry all over again. In all my boyhood life I am not sure that I ever tried to lead a better life in the daytime — or wanted to. In my age I should never think of wishing to do such a thing. But in my age, as in my youth, night brings me a deep sorrow for my deeds. I realize that from babyhood up I have been like the rest of the race — never quite right in the mind at night.

CHAPTER 10

In Hannibal when I was about fifteen I was for a short time a member of a temperance organization. During membership we had to promise not to use tobacco. We would turn out and march with red ribbons around us on May Day with the Sunday schools and on Independence Day with the Sunday schools, the independent fire company, and the soldiers. But you can't keep a boy's moral institution alive on two displays of ribbons a year. I resigned after the two big days.

I had not smoked for three full months and no words can describe the smoke hunger that was eating me up. I had been a smoker from my ninth year — a private one during the first two years but a public one after that — that is to say, after my father's death. In my early manhood and in middle life I used to worry myself with reforms every now and then. I never had occasion to regret these reforms because the rewarding pleasure which I got out of the vice when I returned to it always paid me for all that it cost.

Mark Twain, seated, facing slightly right, holding a pipe.

CHAPTER 11

An exciting event in our village was the arrival of the mesmerizer. I think the year was 1850 when one named Simmons was there. He made public announcement of his show and promised wonders. It cost twenty-five cents to get in, children and Negroes half price. The village had heard of mesmerism in a general way but had not seen it yet. Not many people went the first night but next day they had so many wonders to tell that for a couple of weeks the mesmerizer was making money. I was fourteen or fifteen years old, the age at which a boy will do anything to attract attention to himself. When I saw the "subjects" perform foolishly on the platform and make the people laugh and shout and admire I had a burning desire to be a subject myself.

Every night I sat in the row of candidates on the platform and held the magic disk in my hand and looked at it and tried to get sleepy, but it was a failure; I remained wide awake. On the fourth night I could resist no longer. When I had stared at the disk a while I pretended to be sleepy and began to nod. Straightway came the mesmerizer and made signs with his hands over my head. He took the disk in his fingers and told me that I could not take my eyes off of it, try as I might. I rose slowly and followed that disk all over the place, just as I had seen the others do. Then he put me through some other tricks. Upon suggestion I ran from snakes, passed pails at a fire, made love to imaginary girls, fished from the platform, and so on. I was careful at first and watchful, being afraid the mesmerizer would discover I was just acting and drive me from the platform in shame; but as soon as I realized that I was not in danger I saw more than was to be seen and added details of my own.

"That you may know how wonderfully developed a subject we have in this boy," the mesmerizer said, "I assure you that without a single spoken word to guide him he has carried out what I mentally commanded him to do, to the smallest detail."

I was a hero, and happier than I have ever been in this world since. As regards mental suggestion, my fears of it were gone. I judged that in case I failed to do what the mesmerizer might be willing me to do, I could count on doing something that would answer just as well. I was right, and the mesmerizer, not being a fool, always pretended I was acting out his commands.

After the fourth night I was the only subject. Simmons invited no more candidates to the platform. I performed alone every night for two weeks. When the mesmerizer's engagement closed there was but one person in the village who did not believe in mesmerism and I was the one, and I remained a disbeliever for close upon fifty years. The truth is I did not have to wait long to get tired of my triumphs. Not thirty days, I think. The glory that is built upon a lie becomes nothing but trouble. How easy it is to make people believe a lie and how hard it is to undo that work again! Thirty-five years after my performance I visited my mother, whom I had not seen for ten years. I thought I would confess to her my old dishonesty. It cost me a great effort to make up my mind, but I told her the truth.

She simply did not believe me and said so! I was unhappy not to have my costly truthfulness believed. I kept repeating my statement that every single thing I had done on those long ago nights was a lie. She shook her head calmly and said she knew better. And so the lie which I played upon her in my youth remained with her an absolute truth to the day of her death. Carlyle said "a lie cannot live." It shows that he did not know how to tell them.

CHAPTER 12

Where now is Billy Rice? He was a joy to me and so were the others in the minstrel show who made life a pleasure to me forty years ago and later. They are all, I suppose, departed to return no more for- ever, and with them the real Negro minstrel show, the show which had no equal. We have grand opera and I have seen and greatly enjoyed the first act of everything Wagner created, but the effect on me has always been so powerful that one act was quite sufficient; after two acts I have gone away physically exhausted.

I remember the first minstrel show I ever saw. It must have been in the early 1840s. It was a new institution. In our village of Hannibal we had not heard of it before and it came upon us as a glad and wonderful surprise.

The show remained a week and gave a performance every night. Church members did not attend these performances, but all the other people did — and they loved them.

The original plan of the minstrel show was kept without change for many years. There was no curtain on the stage in the beginning; presently the minstrels came in and took their seats, each with a musical instrument in his hands. In the middle of the group was a very elegantly dressed man, who began with a remark like this:

"I hope, gentlemen, I have the pleasure of seeing you in your usual good health and that everything has gone well with you since we last had the good fortune to meet."

From this point on there would be a steadily growing quarrel between the two on each side of the elegant gentleman, getting louder and louder and finally threatening bloodshed, with the man in the middle meantime begging them to keep the peace and observe good manners, but all in vain, of course. Sometimes the quarrel would last five minutes, the two contestants shouting deadly threats in each other's faces with their noses not six inches apart. Then finally they would back away from each other, each making threats as to what was going to happen to the other the next time they met. Then they would sink back into their chairs and make noises back and forth at each other.

The man in the middle of the row would now make a remark which was intended to remind one of the end men of an experience of his — which it always did. It was usually an experience of a tired sort and as old as America.

The minstrel show was born in the early forties and it had a successful career for about thirty-five years. To my mind it was a thoroughly delightful thing and a most laughter-making one and I am sorry it is gone.

As I have said, it was the non- church people who attended that first minstrel show in Hannibal. Ten or twelve years later the minstrel show was as common in America as the Fourth of July but my mother had never seen one. She was about sixty years old by this time and she came down to St. Louis with a dear and lovely lady of her own age, an old citizen of Hannibal, Aunt Betsey Smith. She wasn't anybody's aunt in particular, she was aunt to the whole town of Hannibal; this was because of her sweet and loving nature.

Like my mother, Aunt Betsey Smith had never seen a minstrel show. She and my mother were very much alive; their age counted for nothing; they were fond of excitement, fond of anything going on that was proper for a member of the church to enjoy. In St. Louis they were eager for something new to see and they asked me for help. They wanted something exciting and proper. I told them I knew of nothing in their line except a meeting in the great hall of the Mercantile Library for an exhibition of native African music. They were charmed with the idea and eager to go. I was not telling them the truth and I knew it at the time, but it was no great matter; it is not worthwhile to try to tell the truth to people who might not believe you even if it is the truth.

The show was the Christy minstrels, in that day one of the most famous and also one of the best. We went early and got seats in the front. By and by, when all the seats on that spacious floor were occupied, there were sixteen hundred persons present. When the Negroes came out on the stage in their extreme costumes, the old ladies were almost speechless. I explained to them that they always dressed like that in Africa. I said that by looking around they could see that the best people in St. Louis were present and that certainly they would not be if the show were not a proper sort.

They were comforted and also quite shamelessly glad to be there. They were happy now; all that they had needed was a pretense of some kind or other to quiet their consciences, and their consciences were quiet now, quiet enough to be dead. The middleman began. Presently he told the first of the old jokes that everybody in the house except my mother and Aunt Betsey had heard a hundred times; a cold silence settled down upon the sixteen hundred. But my two old ladies threw their heads back and went off into wholehearted laughter that so astonished and delighted that great audience that it rose in a solid body to look and see who it might be that had not heard that joke before. The laughter of the two ladies went on and on until the whole sixteen hundred joined in and shook the place with the thunders of their joy.

Aunt Betsey and my mother achieved a brilliant success for the Christy minstrels that night, for all the jokes were as new to them as they were old to the rest of the house. They received them with laughter and they passed the fun along, and the audience left the place weary with laughing and full of thankfulness to the innocent pair who had furnished to their tired souls that rare and precious pleasure.

CHAPTER 13

I LATELY RECEIVED A LETTER FROM ENGLAND FROM A GENTLEMAN whose belief in phrenology is strong and who wonders why phrenology has apparently never interested me enough to move me to write about it. I have explained as follows:

Dear Sir:

I never did study phrenology deeply; therefore I am neither qualified to express an opinion about it nor entitled to do so. In London, thirty-three or thirty-four years ago, I made a small test of phrenology for my better information. I went to Fowler under an assumed name and he examined my elevations and depressions and gave me a report which I carried home and studied with great interest and amusement — the same interest and amusement which I should have found in the report of someone who had been passing himself off as me and who did not resemble me in a single detail. I waited three months and went to Mr. Fowler again. Again I carried away a fancy report. It contained several details of my character (using the same assumed name), but it bore no recognizable resemblance to the earlier report. These experiences gave me feeling against phrenology which has lasted until now.

In America forty or fifty years ago, Fowler and Wells stood at the head of the phrenological industry, and the firm's name was familiar in all ears. Their publications were read and studied and discussed by truth-seekers all over the land. One of the most frequent arrivals in our village of Hannibal was the traveling phrenologist and he was popular and always welcome. He gathered the people together and gave them a free lecture on the wonders of phrenology, then felt their heads and made an estimate of the results, at twenty-five cents per head. I think the people were almost always satisfied with the results.

It is not at all likely, I think, that the traveling expert ever got any villager's character quite right, but it is a safe guess that he was always wise enough to furnish them with reports that would compare favorably with George Washington's.

I was brought up in this atmosphere of faith and belief and trust, and I think its influence was still upon me, so many years afterward, when I saw Fowler's public announcements in London. I was glad to see his name and glad of an opportunity to personally test his art. That I did not give my real name shows that not all the faith of my boyhood was still with me.

Fowler received me with indifference, fingered my head in an uninterested way and named my qualities in a bored voice. He said I possessed surprising courage, great daring, a stern will, a fearlessness without limit. I was astonished at this, and pleased, too. Then he felt the other side of my head and found an elevation there which he called "carefulness." This elevation was so tall, so mountainous, that it reduced my fearlessness one to a mere hill by comparison. He continued his discoveries, with the result that I came out safe and sound, at the end, with a hundred great and shining qualities; but which lost their value and amounted to nothing because each of the hundred was paired with an opposing weakness which took the effectiveness all out of it.

CHAPTER 14

For thirty years I have received an average of a dozen letters a year from strangers who remember me or whose fathers remember me as a boy and young man. But these letters are almost always disappointing. I have not known these strangers nor their fathers. I have not heard of the names they mention; the memories which they call to my attention have had no part in my experience; all of which means that these strangers have been mistaking me for somebody else. But I received this morning a letter from a man who deals in names that were familiar to me in my boyhood. The letter read:

You no doubt are at a loss to know who I am. I will tell you. In my younger days I lived in Hannibal, Missouri, and you and I were schoolmates attending Mr. Dawson's school along with Sam and Will Bowen and Andy Fuqua and others whose names I have forgotten. I was then about the smallest boy in school, for my age, and they called me little Aleck Tonkray for short.

I don't remember Aleck Tonkray but I knew those other people as well as I knew the town drunkards. I remember Dawson's schooling perfectly. I can remember the sleepy and inviting summer sounds that used to drift in through the open windows. I remember Andy Fuqua, the oldest pupil — a man of twenty- five. I remember Mr. Dawson very well, I remember his boy, Theodore, who was as good as he could be.
In fact he was too good, hatefully good, and I would have drowned him if I had a chance. In this school we were all about on an equality, and so far as I remember, envy had no place in our hearts except in the case of Arch Fuqua — the other one's brother. Of course we all went bare- foot in the summertime. Arch Fuqua was about my own age — ten or eleven. In the winter we could stand him, because he wore shoes then, and his great gift was hidden from our sight and we could forget it. But in the summertime he was our envy, for he could double back his big toe and let it fly and you could hear it snap for thirty yards. There was not another boy in the school that could approach this trick. Except Theodore Eddy who could make his ears go back and forth like a horse's. But he was no real rival, for you couldn't hear him move his ears; so all the advantage lay with Arch Fuqua.

George RoBards, eighteen or twenty years old, was the only pupil who studied Latin. He was a fine young fellow in all ways. He and Mary Moss were sweethearts from a time when they were merely children. But a Mr. Lakeman arrived now to live in the town. He took an important position in that little town at once and kept it. He brought with him a distinguished reputation as a lawyer. He was educated, cultured, brave and dignified. He was a rising man and a bachelor. As a catch he stood at the top of the market. That blooming and beautiful thing, Mary Moss, attracted his favor. He sought her hand and won. Everyone said she accepted him to please her parents, not herself. They were married. And everybody then said he continued her schooling all by himself, proposing to educate her up to standard and make her a suitable companion for him. These things may have been true. They might not have been true. But they were interesting. That is the main requirement in a village like that. George went away, presently, to some far-off region and there he died — of a broken heart, everybody said. That could be true, for he had good cause. He would go far before he would find another Mary Moss.

How long ago that little tragedy happened! None but the white-haired knows about it now. Lakeman is dead these many years but Mary still lives and is still beautiful, although she has grandchildren.

John RoBards was the little brother of George. When he was twelve years old he crossed the country with his father during the rush of the gold seekers of 1849 and I can remember the departure of the men and horses westward. We were all there to see and to envy. And I can still see that proud boy sailing on a great horse, with his long golden hair streaming out behind. We were all on hand to gaze and envy when he returned two years later in unimaginable glory — for he had traveled! None of us had ever been forty miles from home. But he had crossed the continent. He had been in the gold mines, that fairy land of our imagination. And he had done a still more wonderful thing. He had been in ships — in ships on the actual ocean; in ships on three actual oceans. We would have sold our souls to Satan for the privilege of trading places with him.

I saw him when I was out on that Missouri trip four years ago. He was old then though not quite so old as I — and the sorrows of life were upon him. He said that his granddaughter, twelve years old, had read my books and would like to see me. It was a sad time, for she was a prisoner in her room and marked for death. And John knew that she was passing swiftly away. Twelve years old — just her grandfather's age when he rode away on that great journey. In her I seemed to see that boy again. She had heart disease and her brief life came to a close a few days later.

Another of those schoolboys was John Garth. And one of the prettiest of the schoolgirls was Helen Kercheval. They grew up and married. He became a wealthy banker and a leading and valued citi- zen; and a few years ago he died, rich and honored. He died. It is what I have to say about so many of those boys and girls. The widow still lives, and there are grandchildren.

Will Bowen was another schoolmate and so was his brother, Sam, who was his junior by a couple of years. Before the Civil War broke out both became St. Louis and New Orleans pilots. Both are dead, long ago. While Sam was still very young he had a curious adventure. He fell in love with a girl of sixteen, only child of a wealthy German. He wanted to marry her but he and she both thought that the father would not only not consent but would shut his door against Sam. The old man would not have, but they were not aware of that. He had his eye upon them and it was not an unfriendly eye. But the young couple got to living together in secret. Before long the old man died. When the will was examined it was found that he had left the whole of his wealth to Mrs. Samuel A. Bowen. Then the poor things made another mistake. They rushed down to Carondelet, outside the city, and got a judge to marry them and date the marriage back a few months. The old German had some nieces and nephews and cousins and they traced out the trickery and proved it and got the property. This left Sam with a girl wife on his hands and the necessity of earning a living for her at the pilot wheel. After a few years Sam and another pilot were bringing a boat up from New Orleans when the yellow fever broke out. Both pilots were stricken with it and there was nobody to take their place at the wheel. The boat was landed at the head of an island to wait for help. Death came swiftly to both pilots and there they lie buried, unless the river has cut the graves away and washed the bones into the stream, a thing which probably happened long ago.

CHAPTER 15

In 1845, WHEN I WAS ten years old, there was an outbreak of measles in the town and it made a most alarming killing among the little people. There was a funeral almost daily and the mothers of the town were nearly mad with fright. My mother was greatly troubled. She worried over Pamela and Henry and me and took constant and extraordinary pains to keep us from coming into contact with the dis- ease. I believed that her judgment was at fault. I cannot remember now whether I was frightened about the measles or not but I clearly remember that I grew very tired of being continually under the threat of death. I remember I got so weary of it and so eager to have the matter settled one way or the other and promptly that this worry spoiled my days and nights. I had no pleasure in them. I made up my mind to settle this matter one way or the other and be done with it.

Will Bowen was dangerously ill with the measles and I thought I would go down there and catch them. I entered the house by the front way and slipped along through rooms and halls, keeping sharp watch against discovery, and at last I reach Will's bedroom in the rear of the house on the second floor and got into it uncaptured. But that was as far as my victory reached. His mother caught me there a moment later and gave me a lecture and drove me away. I saw that I must manage better next time and I did. I hung about the lane at the rear of the house and watched through cracks in the fence until I was convinced conditions were favorable. Then I slipped through the back yard and up the back way and got into the room and into the bed with Will Bowen without being observed. I don't know how long I was in the bed. I only remember that Will Bowen, as society, had no value for me, for he was too sick to even notice that I was there. When I heard his mother coming, I covered up my head, but it was summertime — that cover was nothing more than a sheet, and anybody could see that there were two of us under it. It didn't remain two very long. Mrs. Bowen pulled me out of that bed and took me home herself, with a hold on my collar which she never loosened until she delivered me into my mother's hands along with her opinion of that kind of boy.

It was a good case of measles that resulted. It brought me within a shade of death's door. It brought me to where I no longer felt any interest in anything, but instead felt a total absence of interest — which was sweet and delightful. I have never enjoyed anything in my life any more than I enjoyed dying that time.

CHAPTER 16

One day recently a chance remark called to my mind an early sweetheart of mine and I fell to talking about her. I hadn't seen her for forty- eight years; but no matter, I found that I remembered her quite clearly and that she possessed a lively interest for me notwithstanding that great interval of time. She wasn't yet fifteen when I knew her. It was in the summertime and she had gone down the Mississippi from St. Louis to New Orleans as a guest of a relative of hers who was a pilot on the John]. Roe, a steamboat whose officers I knew very well, as I had served a term in that boat's pilothouse. She was a freighter, but she always had a dozen passengers on board; they paid no fare; they were guests of the captain and nobody was responsible for them if anything of a fatal nature happened to them.

It was a delightful old boat and she had a very spacious deck — just the place for moonlight dancing and daytime fun, and such things were always happening. She was a charmingly slow boat. Mark Leavenworth, her captain, was a giant, and warm-hearted and good-natured, which is the way with giants. Zeb, his brother, was another giant, possessed of the same qualities, and of a laugh which could be heard from Vicksburg to Nebraska. He was one of the pilots and Beck Jolly was another.

Jolly was very handsome, very graceful, very intelligent, companionable — a fine character — and he had the manners of a duke.

Beck Jolly was a beautiful creature to look at. But it's different now. I saw him four years ago and he had white hair, and not much of it, and two sets of cheeks and chins.

All the crew were simple-hearted folk and overflowing with good-fellowship and the milk of human kindness. They had all been reared on farms in the interior of Indiana and they had brought the simple farm ways and farm spirit to that steamboat. When she was on a voyage there was nothing in her to suggest a steamboat. One didn't seem to be on board a steamboat at all. He was floating around on a farm. Nothing in this world pleasanter than this can be imagined.

At the time I speak of I had fallen out of the heaven of the John J. Roe and was steering for Brown, on the swift passenger boat Pennsylvania. On a memorable trip, the Pennsylvania arrived at New Orleans, and I discovered that she was in the harbor right next to the John J. Roe. I climbed over the rail and jumped aboard the Roe, landing on that spacious deck of hers. It was like arriving home at the farmhouse after a long absence. As usual, there were a dozen passengers, male and female, young and old; as usual they were of the likable sort affected by the John J. Roe farmers. Now, out of their midst, floating upon my vision, came that slender girl of whom I have spoken — that instantly elected sweet- heart out of far-away Missouri — a frank and simple child who had never been away from home in her life before, and had brought with her to these distant regions the freshness of her own land.

I can state the rest, I think, in a very few words. I was not four inches from the girl's side during our waking hours for the next three days. Then there came a sudden interruption. Zeb Leavenworth came aboard shouting, "The Pennsylvania is backing out." I fled at my best speed, made a flying leap, and just managed to make the connection, and nothing to spare.

That charming child was Laura M. Wright, and I could see her with perfect distinctness when I was telling about it last Saturday. And I finished with the remark, "I never saw her afterward. It is now forty-eight years, one month and twenty-seven days since that parting, and no word has ever passed between us since."

I reached home from Fairhaven last Wednesday and found a let- ter from Laura Wright. It shook me to the foundations. In the place of that carefree girl of forty- eight years ago, I imagined the world-worn and trouble -worn widow of sixty-two. Laura's letter was an appeal to me for money for herself and for her disabled son, who, as she mentioned, is thirty-seven years old. She is in need of a thousand dollars and I sent it.

It is an awful world — it is a devilish world. When I knew that child her father was an honored judge of a high court and was a rich man, as riches were counted in that day. What had that girl done, what crime had she committed that she must be punished with poverty in her old age?

We have heard again from my long vanished little fourteen-year-old sweetheart. She has written a charming letter and it is full of character. I find in her, once more at sixty-two, the little girl of fourteen of so long ago. Her letter carried me back so far into the past that for the moment I was living it over again, the stretch of years between forgotten. And so, when I presently came upon the following in her letter it hit me with surprise and seemed to be referring to some- body else:

But I must not weary you nor take up your valuable time. I really forget that I am writing to one of the world's most famous and sought-after men.

And so I am a hero to Laura Wright! It is wholly unthinkable. One can be a hero to other folk, and in a sort of way understand it, or at least believe it, but that a person can really be a hero to a near and familiar friend is a thing which no hero has ever yet been able to realize, I am sure.

CHAPTER 17

I WAS EDUCATED NOT ONLY IN THE COMMON SCHOOL AT HANNIBAL, but also in my brother Orion's newspaper office. Orion was the family's first-born. When he was fifteen or sixteen he was sent to St. Louis and there he learned the printer's trade.

Mark Twain's oldest brother, Orion Clemens.

One of his characteristics was eagerness. He woke with an eagerness about some matter or other every morning; it drove him all day; it died in the night and he was on fire with a fresh new interest next morning before he could get his clothes on. But I am forgetting another characteristic, a very pronounced one. That was his deep despairs; these had their place in each and every day along with the eagerness. Thus his day was divided from sunrise to mid- night with first brilliant sunshine and then black clouds. Every day he was the most joyous and hopeful man that ever was, I think, and also every day he was the most miserable man that ever was.

He joined a number of churches, one after another, and taught in the Sunday schools — changing his Sunday school every time he changed his religion. He changed his politics too — Whig today, Democrat next week, and anything fresh he could find in the political market the week after. Throughout his long life he was always changing religions and enjoying the change of scenery. Notwithstanding, his honesty was never questioned. His principles were always high and absolutely unshakable. You could lower his spirits with a single word; you could raise them into the sky again with another one. You could break his heart with a word of disapproval; you could make him as happy as an angel with a word of approval. He was always truthful; he was always free from deceit; he was always honest and honorable. But in light matters — like religion and politics and such things — he never had a belief that could remain alive after a disapproving remark from a cat.

He was always dreaming; he was a dreamer from birth and this characteristic got him into trouble now and then. Once when he was twenty-three or twenty-four years old he thought of the romantic idea of coming to Hannibal from St. Louis without giving us notice, in order that he might give the family a pleasant surprise. If he had given notice he would have been informed that we had moved and that that old deep -voiced sailorman, Doctor Meredith, our family physician, was living in the house which we had formerly occupied and that Orion's former room in that house was now occupied by Doctor Meredith's two ripe old-maid sisters. Orion arrived at Hannibal in the middle of the night. When he arrived at the house he went around to the back door and slipped off his boots and crept upstairs and arrived at the room of those old maids without having wakened any sleepers. He undressed in the dark and got into bed and crowded up against somebody. He was a little surprised, but not much, for he thought it was our brother Ben. It was winter and the bed was comfortable and the supposed Ben added to the comfort — and he was dropping off to sleep very well satisfied with his progress so far and full of happy dreams of what was going to hap- pen in the morning. But something else was going to happen sooner than that, and it happened now. The old maid that was being crowded presently came to a half-waking condition and protested against the crowding. She felt around and found Orion's beard and screamed, "Why, it's a man!" Orion was out of the bed and hunting around in the dark for his clothes. He did not wait to get his whole outfit. He started with such parts of it as he could find. He flew to the head of the
stairs and started down. Then he saw the faint yellow flame of a candle coming up the stairs from below. Doctor Meredith was behind it.

He had no clothes on to speak of, but no matter, he was well enough fixed for an occasion like this, because he had a butcher knife in his hand. Orion shouted to him and this saved his life, for the doctor recognized his voice. Then, in those deep tones of his that I used to admire so much when I was a little boy, he explained to Orion the change that had been made, told him where to find the Clemens family, and closed with some quite unnecessary advice about checking in advance before he undertook another adventure like that — advice which Orion probably never needed again as long as he lived.

CHAPTER 18

My father died in 1847, just at the very moment when our fortunes had changed and we were about to be comfortable once more after several years of poverty which had been brought on us by the dishonest act of one Ira Stout, to whom my father had loaned several thousand dollars — a fortune in those days. My father had just been elected clerk of the Surrogate Court. This modest prosperity was not only quite sufficient for us and for our ambitions, but he was held in such high regard and honor throughout the county that his occupancy of that dignified office would, in the opinion of everybody, be his possession as long as he might live. He went to Palmyra County seat about the end of February. In returning home, twelve miles by horseback, a cold rainstorm soaked him and he arrived at the house in a half-frozen condition. He died on the 24th of March.

Thus our splendid new fortune was taken away from us and we were in the depths of poverty again. It is the way such things are accustomed to happen.

Orion did not come to Hannibal until two or three years after my father's death. He remained in St. Louis. Out of his wage as a printer he supported my mother and my brother Henry, who was two years younger than I. My sister Pamela helped in this support by taking piano pupils. Thus we got along, but it was pretty hard going. I was not one of the problems, because I was taken from school at once upon my father's death and placed in the office of the newspaper, the Hannibal Courier, as printer's apprentice. Mr. Ament, the editor and owner of the paper, allowed me the usual pay of the office of apprentice — that is to say, board and clothes but no money. The clothes consisted of two suits a year but one of the suits always failed to materialize and the other suit was not purchased so long as Mr. Ament's old clothes held out. I was only about half as big as Ament, so his shirts gave me the uncomfortable sense of living in a tent.

CHAPTER 19

It was during my first year's apprenticeship in the Courier office that I did a thing which I have been trying to regret for fifty-five years. It was a summer afternoon and just the kind of weather that a boy prizes for river trips and other fun, but I was a prisoner. The others were all gone holidaying. I was alone and sad. I had committed a crime of some sort and this was the punishment. I must lose my holiday and spend the afternoon alone besides. I had one comfort and it was a generous one while it lasted. It was the half of a long and broad watermelon, fresh and red and ripe. I dug it out with a knife and I found room for it in my person — though it did crowd me until the juice ran out of my ears. There remained then the shell, the hollow shell. I didn't want to waste it and I couldn't think of anything to do with it that afforded entertainment. I was sitting at the open window which looked out upon the sidewalk of the main street three stories below, when it occurred to me to drop it on somebody's head. I doubted the wisdom of this, because so much of the resulting entertainment would fall to my share and so little to the other person's. But I thought I would chance it.

I watched out of the window for the right person to come along — the safe person — but he didn't come. But at last I saw the right one coming. It was my brother Henry. He was the best boy in the whole region. He never did harm to anybody. He had an overflowing amount of goodness — but not enough to save him this time. I watched his approach with eager interest. He came walking slowly along, dreaming his pleasant summer dream. When he was almost under me all I could see from my high place was the end of his nose and his feet. Then I placed the watermelon, figured my distance and let it go, hollow side down.

My aim was beyond admiration. The shell landed right on the top of his head. I wanted to go down there and tell him I was sorry but it would not have been safe. He would have known I had done it. He said nothing about this adventure for two or three days — I was watching him in the meantime to keep out of danger — and I was deceived into believing he had no suspicion.

It was a mistake. He was only waiting for a sure opportunity. Then he landed a rock on the side of my head which raised a swelling so large I had to wear two hats for a time. I carried this crime to my mother, for I was always anxious to get Henry into trouble with her and could never succeed. I thought that I had a sure case this time. I showed the swelling to her but she said it was no matter. She didn't need to inquire into the circumstances. She knew I deserved it, and the best way would be for me to accept it as a valuable lesson and thereby get profit out of it.

About 1849 or 1850 Orion broke his connection with the printing-house in St. Louis and came up to Hannibal and bought a weekly paper called the Hannibal Journal for the sum of five hundred dollars cash. He took me out of the Courier office and hired me at three and a half a week, which was an extraordinary wage, but Orion was always generous with everybody but himself. It cost him nothing in my case, for he was never able to pay me a single penny as long as I was with him. By the end of the first year he found that he must cut down. The office rent was cheap but it was not cheap enough. He could not afford to pay rent of any kind, so he moved the whole plant into the house we lived in. He kept that paper alive during four years but I have at this time no idea how he did it.

Finally he handed it over to Mr. Johnson, from whom he had borrowed the money to buy it, and went to Muscatine, Iowa, and bought a small interest in a weekly newspaper there.

Mark Twain, seated, reading a newspaper.

I had not joined the Muscatine venture. Just before that happened (which I think was in 1853) I disappeared one night and fled to St. Louis. There I worked at the Evening News for a time and then started on my travels to see the world. The world was New York City and there was a little World's Fair there. I arrived in New York with two or three dollars in pocket change and a ten-dollar bank bill concealed in the lining of my coat. I got work at murderous wages, just enough to pay for board and room. By and by I went to Philadelphia and worked some months.

Finally I made a trip to Washington to see the sights, and in 1854 I went back to the Mississippi Valley. I worked in a little printing office in Keokuk, Iowa, where Orion had now gone, for two years. Then I worked on board the swift and popular New Orleans and St. Louis boat, Pennsylvania. I was in New Orleans when Louisiana went out of the Union, January 26, 1861, and I started north the next day.

By this time Orion was very hard-pressed for money. But I was beginning to earn a wage of two hundred and fifty dollars a month as a pilot and so I supported him until his old friend, Edward Bates, then a member of Mr. Lincoln's first Cabinet, got him the place of Secretary of the new Territory of Nevada, and Orion and I headed for that country. At first I went about the country seeking silver, but at the end of '62 or the beginning of '63 I went to work on a newspaper in Virginia City, Nevada, the Enterprise.

I was sent down to Carson City to report the legislative meetings. I wrote a weekly letter to the paper; it appeared Sundays and as a result on Monday the legislative proceedings were stopped short by the complaints of the members. They answered the correspondent with anger, describing him with long fancy phrases, for lack of a briefer way. To save their time, I presently began to sign the letters "Mark Twain" (two fathoms — twelve feet), the Mississippi river boatman's call for announcing the depth of the water.

Then after two years on the Enterprise I went west to California.

CHAPTER 20

I WAS A REPORTER ON THE MORNING CALL OF SAN FRANCISCO. I WAS

more than that — I was the reporter. There was no other. There was enough work for one and a little over, but not enough for two — according to Mr. Barnes's idea, and he was the owner and therefore in the best place to know.

By nine in the morning I had to be at the police court for an hour and make a brief history of the fights of the night before. They were usually between Irishmen and Irishmen, and Chinamen and Chinamen, with now and then a fight between the two races for a change. Each day's evidence was just like the evidence of the day before, therefore the daily performance was killingly dull. All the courts came under the head of the reporter "regulars." They were sources of information which never failed. During the rest of the day we combed the two from end to end, gathering such material as we might, wherewith to fill our required column — and if there were no fires to report we started some.

At night we visited the six theaters, one after the other; seven nights in the week, three hundred and sixty-five nights in the year. We remained in each of those places five minutes, got the merest passing glimpse of plays and operas, and we "wrote up" those plays and operas, as the phrase goes, every night from the beginning of the year to the end of it, trying to find something to say about those performances which we had not said a couple of hundred times before.

After having been hard at work from nine or ten in the morning until eleven at night getting material together somehow, I took the pen and spread it out in words and phrases and made it cover as much ground as I could. It was fearful, soulless work and almost completely lacking in interest. It was awful slavery for a lazy man, and I was born lazy. I am no lazier now than I was forty years ago, but that is because I reached the limit forty years ago. You can't go beyond possibility.

I was higher-toned forty years ago than I am now and I felt a deep shame in my situation as slave of such a newspaper as the Morning Call. If I had been still higher-toned I would have thrown up my job and gone out and starved, like any other hero. But I had never had any experience at being a hero. I had dreamed of heroism, like everybody, but I had had no practice and I didn't know how to begin. I couldn't stand to begin with starving. I had already come near to that once or twice in my life and got no real enjoyment out of remembering about it. I knew I couldn't get another job if I resigned. I knew it perfectly well. Therefore I swallowed my pride and stayed where I was. But whereas there had been little enough interest in my industries before, there was none at all now. I continued my work but I took not the least interest in it, and naturally there were results. I got to neglecting it. As I have said, there was too much of it for one man. The way I was conducting it now, there was apparently work enough in it for two or three. Even Barnes noticed that, and told me to get an assistant, on half wages.

There was a man down in the counting room — good-natured, obliging, unintelligent— and he was getting little or nothing a week. He was a graceless boy who had no feeling for anybody or anything. He was called Smiggy McGlural. I offered the job of assistant to Smiggy and he accepted it with gratefulness. He went at his work with ten times the energy that was left in me. He was not intelligent, but this quality was not required or needed in a Morning Call reporter and so he conducted his office to perfection. I gradually got to leaving more and more of the work to McGlural. I grew lazier and lazier and within thirty days he was doing almost the whole of it. It was also plain that he could accomplish the whole of it and more all by himself and therefore had no real need of me.

Mr. Barnes discharged me. It was the only time in my life that I have ever been discharged and it hurts yet — and I am nearly in my grave. He did not discharge me rudely. It was not in his nature to do that. He was a large, handsome man, with a kindly face and courteous ways, and was faultless in his dress. He could not have said a rude, ungentle thing to anybody. He took me privately aside and advised me to resign. It was like a father advising a son for his good, and I obeyed.

CHAPTER 21

I LEARNED THAT JIM GILLIS IS DEAD. HE DIED, AGED SEVENTY-SEVEN, in California about two weeks ago, after a long illness. I think Jim Gillis was a much more remarkable person than his family and friends ever suspected. He had a bright and smart imagination and it was of the kind that turns out work well and with ease and without previous preparation, just builds a story as it goes along, careless of where it is proceeding, enjoying each fresh fancy as it comes into his mind and caring not at all whether the story shall ever end brilliantly and satisfactorily or not end at all. Jim was born a humorist and a very good one. When I remember how successful were his untrained efforts, I feel sure that he would have been a star performer if he had been discovered and had been subjected to a few years of training with a pen. A genius is not very likely to ever discover himself; neither is he very likely to be discovered by his friends; they are so close to him that they can't see him clearly.

St. Peter's cannot be impressive for size to a person who has always seen it close at hand, and has never been outside of Rome; it is only the stranger, approaching from far away in the Campagna, who sees Rome as an indistinct and characterless mass, with the mighty St. Peter's standing up out of it all, lonely in its majesty.

I spent three months in the home of Jim Gillis and his friend Dick Stoker in Jackass Gulch, that calm and dreamy and lovely paradise. Every now and then Jim would have an idea and he would stand up before the great log fire and deliver himself of an unplanned lie — a fairy story, a romance — with Dick Stoker as the hero of it as a general thing. Jim always soberly pretended that what he was telling was actually history, true history, not romance. Dick Stoker, gray- headed and good-natured, would sit, smoking his pipe, and listen with a gentle air to these big lies and never deny their truth.

Once or twice Jim's lively imagination got him into trouble. An Indian woman came along one day and tried to sell us some wild fruit that looked like apples. Dick Stoker had lived nearby for eighteen years and knew that this fruit was worthless and could not be eaten; but carelessly and without purpose he remarked that he had never heard of it before. That was enough for Jim. He started to praise that devilish fruit, and the more he talked about it the warmer and stronger his admiration of it grew. He said that he had eaten it a thousand times; that all one needed to do was to boil it with a little sugar and there was nothing in America that could compare with it for deliciousness. He was only talking to hear himself talk; and so he was brought up standing and for just one moment, or maybe two moments, struck dumb when Dick interrupted him with the remark that if the fruit was so delicious why didn't he buy some right now. Jim was caught but he wouldn't show it; he was not the man to back down or confess; he pretended that he was only too happy to have this chance to enjoy once more this precious gift of God. Oh, he was a man true to his statements! I think he would have eaten that fruit if he had known it would kill him. He bought it all and said airily that he was glad enough to have that blessing and that if Dick and I didn't want to enjoy it with him we could let it alone — he didn't care.

Then there followed a couple of the most delightful hours I have ever spent. Jim took a very large empty can and put it on the fire and filled it half full of water and put into it a dozen of those devilish fruits; and as soon as the water came to a good boil he added a handful of sugar; as the boiling went on he tasted the smelly stuff from time to time; and now he began to make tests with a tablespoon. He would dip out a spoonful and taste it, remark that perhaps it needed a little more sugar — so he would throw in a handful and let the boiling go on a while longer; handful after handful of sugar went in and still the tasting went on for two hours.

At last he said the manufacture had reached the right stage, the stage of perfection. He dipped his spoon, tasted, and broke into enthusiasms of grateful joy; then he gave us a taste apiece. From all that we could discover, those pounds and pounds of sugar had not affected the fruit's evil sharpness in the least degree. Acid? It was all acid, with not a trace of the sweetness which the sugar ought to have given to it if that fruit had been invented anywhere outside of hell. We stopped with that one taste, but that great-hearted Jim went on eating and eating and eating, and praising and praising and praising, until his teeth and tongue were raw, and Stoker and I nearly dead with thankfulness and delight. During the next two days neither food nor drink passed Jim's teeth; so sore were they that they could not endure the touch of anything, even his breath passing over them hurt; nevertheless he went steadily on voicing his admiration of that awful stuff and praising God. It was an astonishing show of bravery.

I mourn for Jim. He was a good man and firm friend, a manly one, a generous one; an honest and honorable man and gifted with a lovable nature. He picked no fights himself but when a fight was put upon him he was there and ready.

CHAPTER 22

My experiences as an author began early in 1867. 1 came to New York from San Francisco in the first month of that year and presently Charles H. Webb, whom I had known in San Francisco as a reporter on The Bulletin and afterwards editor of The Californian, suggested that I publish a volume of sketches. I was charmed and excited by the suggestion and quite willing to try it if some industrious person would save me the trouble of gathering the sketches together. I didn't want to do it myself, for from the beginning there has been an empty spot in me where the industry ought to be.

Webb undertook to assemble the sketches. He performed this office, then handed the result to me and I went to his publisher's, Carleton's, establishment with it. I approached a clerk and he bent eagerly over the counter to inquire into my needs; but when he found that I had come to sell a book and not to buy one, his temperature fell sixty degrees. I asked the privilege of a word with Mr. Carleton and was coldly informed that he was in his private office. But after a while I got by the clerk and entered the holy of holies. Ah, now I remember how I managed it! Webb had made an appointment for me with Carleton. Carleton rose and said in a not very inviting manner, "Well, what can I do for you?"

I reminded him that I was there by appointment to offer him my book for publication. He began to swell and went on swelling and swelling and swelling until he had reached the size of a god of about the second or third degree. Then the fountains of his great deep were broken up and for two or three minutes I couldn't see him for the rain.
It was words, only words, but they fell so thickly that they darkened the atmosphere. Finally he made an important sweep with his right hand which took in the whole room, and said:

"Books — look around you! Every place are books that are waiting for publication. Do I want any more? Excuse me, I don't. Good morning."

Twenty-one years went by before I saw Carleton again. I was then staying with my family in Lucerne. He called on me, shook hands in a friendly way and said:

"I am really an unimportant person but I have a couple of such major distinctions to my credit that I am entitled to immortality. I refused a book of yours and for this I stand without competition as the prize fool of the nineteenth century."

It was a most handsome thing for him to apologize and I told him so and said it was sweet to me because during the past twenty-one years I had in fancy taken his life several times every year and always in new and increasingly cruel inhuman ways, but that now I should hold him my true and valued friend and never kill him again.

I reported my adventure to Webb and he bravely said that not all the Carletons in the world should defeat that book, he would publish it himself on a ten percent royalty. And so he did. He brought it out in blue and gold and made a very pretty little book of it. I think he named it The Celebrated Jumping Frog of Calaveras County, and Other Sketches, price $1.25.

In June I sailed in the Quaker City excursion. I returned in November and found a letter from the American Publishing Company of Hartford offering me five percent royalty on a book which would tell the adventures of the excursion. Instead of the royalty I was offered the choice of ten thousand dollars cash upon delivery of my story. I consulted A. D. Richardson and he said, "Take the royalty." I followed his advice and closed the deal.

I was out of money and I went down to Washington to see if I could earn enough there to keep me in bread and butter while I wrote the book. I came across William Swinton, brother of the historian, and together we invented a scheme: we became the fathers and originators of what is a common feature in the newspaper world now, the syndicate. We became the old original first newspaper syndicate in the world; it was on a small scale but that is usual with untried new enterprises. We had twelve journals on our list; they were all weeklies, unknown and poor and scattered far away in the settlements. It was a proud thing for those little newspapers to have a Washington correspondent and a fortunate thing for us that they felt in that way about it. Each of the twelve took two letters a week from us, at a dollar per letter; each of us wrote one letter per week and sent off twelve copies of it to the journals, thus getting twenty-four dollars a week to live on, which was all we needed in our cheap and humble quarters.

Swinton was one of the dearest and loveliest human beings I have ever known, and we led a charmed existence together, in unlimited contentment. Swinton was a gentleman by nature and upbringing; he was highly educated; he was of a beautiful spirit; he was pure in heart and speech. He was a Scotchman and a Presbyterian; a Presbyterian of the old and real school, being honest and true to his religion and lov- ing it and finding peace in it. He hadn't a vice, unless a large and grateful sympathy with Scotch whisky may be called by that name. I didn't regard it as a vice, because he was a Scotchman, and Scotch whisky to a Scotchman is as innocent as milk is to the rest of the human race. In Swinton's case it was a virtue but an expensive one. Twenty-four dollars a week would really have been riches to us if we hadn't had to support that bottle; because of the bottle any lateness in the arrival of any part of our income was sure to cause some inconvenience.

I remember a time when a shortage occurred; we had to have three dollars and we had to have it before the close of the day. I don't know now how we happened to want all that money at one time; I only know we had to have it. Swinton told me to go out and find it and he said he would also go out and see what he could do. He didn't seem to have any doubt that we would succeed but I knew that that was his religion working in him; I hadn't the same confidence; I hadn't any idea where to turn to raise all that money, and I said so. I think he was ashamed of me, privately, because of my weak faith. He told me to give myself no uneasiness, no concern; and said in a simple, confident and unquestioning way, "The Lord will provide." I saw that he fully believed the Lord would provide but it seemed to me that if he had had my experience — but never mind that; before he was done with me his strong faith had had its influence and I went forth from the place almost convinced that the Lord really would provide.

I wandered around the streets for an hour, trying to think up some way to get that money, but nothing suggested itself. At last I walked into the Ebbitt Hotel, and sat down. Presently a dog came over to me. He paused, glanced up at me and said with his eyes, "Are you friendly?" I answered with my eyes that I was. He waved his tail happily and came forward and rested his head on my knee and lifted his brown eyes to my face in a loving way. He was a charming creature, as beautiful as a girl, and he was all made of silk and velvet. I stroked his smooth brown head and we were a pair of lovers right away. Pretty soon Brig. Gen. Miles, the hero of the land, came walking by in his blue and gold uniform, with everybody's admiring gaze upon him. He saw the dog and stopped, and there was a light in his eye which showed that he had a warm place in his heart for dogs like this gracious creature; then he came forward and patted the dog and said:

"He is very fine — he is a wonder; would you sell him?"

I was greatly moved; it seemed a marvelous thing to me, the way Swinton's faith had worked out.

I said, "Yes."

The General said, "What do you ask for him?" "Three dollars."

The General was obviously surprised. He said, "Three dollars? Only three dollars? Why that dog is a most uncommon dog; he can't possibly be worth less than fifty. If he were mine, I wouldn't take a hundred for him. I am afraid you are not aware of his value. Reconsider your price if you like. I don't wish to wrong you. "

But if he had known me he would have known that I was no more capable of wronging him than he was of wronging me. I replied:

"No, three dollars. That is his price."

"Very well, since you insist upon it," said the General, and he gave me three dollars and led the dog away and disappeared upstairs.

In about ten minutes a gentle -faced, middle-aged gentleman came along and began to look around here and there and under tables and everywhere and I said to him, "Is it a dog you are looking for?"

His face had been sad before and troubled; but it lit up gladly now and he answered, "Yes — have you seen him?"

"Yes," I said, "he was here a minute ago and I saw him follow a gentleman away. I think I could find him for you if you would like me to try."

I have seldom seen a person look so grateful. He said that he would like me to try. I said I would do it with great pleasure but that as it might take a little time I hoped he would not mind paying me something for my trouble. He said he would do it most gladly — repeating that phrase "most gladly" — and asked me how much.

I said, "Three dollars."

He looked surprised, and said, "Dear me, it is nothing! I will pay you ten, quite willingly."

But I said, " No, three is the price," and I started for the stairs without waiting for any further argument, for Swinton had said that that was the amount the Lord would provide and it seemed to me that it would be wrong to take a penny more than was promised.

I got the number of the General's room from the office clerk and when I reached the room I found the General there petting his dog and quite happy. I said, "I am sorry, but I have to take the dog again."

He seemed very much surprised and said, "Take him again? Why, he is my dog; you sold him to me and at your own price."

"Yes," I said, "it is true — but I have to have him, because the man wants him again."

"What man?"

"The man that owns him; he wasn't my dog."

The General looked even more surprised than before, and for a moment he couldn't seem to find his voice; then he said, "Do you mean to tell me that you were selling another man's dog — and knew it?"

"Yes, I knew it wasn't my dog."

"Then why did you sell him?"

I said, "Well, that is a curious question to ask. I sold him because you wanted him. You offered to buy the dog; you can't deny that. I was not anxious to sell him — I had not even thought of selling him, but it seemed to me that — "

He broke me off in the middle and said, "It is the most extraordinary thing I have ever heard of — the idea of your selling a dog that didn't belong to you — "

I broke him off there and said, "You said yourself that the dog was probably worth a hundred dollars. I only asked you three; was there anything unfair about that? You offered to pay more, you know you did. I only asked you three; you can't deny it."

"Oh, what in the world has that to do with it! The truth of the matter is that you didn't own the dog — can't you see that? You seem to think that there is nothing wrong in selling properly that isn't yours provided you sell it cheap. Now then — "

I said, "Please don't argue any more about it. You can't get around the fact that the price was perfectly fair, perfectly reasonable — considering that I didn't own the dog — and so arguing about it is only a waste of words. I have to have him back again because the man wants him; don't you see that I haven't any choice in the matter? Put yourself in my place. Suppose you had sold a dog that didn't belong to you; suppose you — "

"Oh," he said, "don't mix me up any more with your crazy reasonings! Take him along and give me a rest."

So I paid back the three dollars and led the dog downstairs and passed him over to his owner and collected three for my trouble.

I went away then with a good conscience, because I had acted honorably; I never could have used the three that I sold the dog for, because it was not rightly my own, but the three I got for returning him to his rightful owner was rightly and properly mine, because I had earned it. That man might never have gotten that dog back at all, if it hadn't been for me. My principles have remained to this day what they were then. I was always honest; I know I can never be otherwise. It is as I said in the beginning — I was never able to persuade myself to use money which I had acquired in questionable ways.

Now then, that is the tale. Some of it is true.

CHAPTER 23

In the beginning of February 1870 I was married to Miss Olivia L. Langdon and moved to Buffalo, New York. Tomorrow will be the thirty- sixth anniversary of our marriage. My wife passed from this life one year and eight months ago in Florence, Italy, after an unbroken illness of twenty-two months.

Mark Twain's wife, Olivia L. Clemens, (picture was taken in 1869, when she was 24).

I saw her first in the form of a small statue in her brother Charley's room on the steamer Quaker City in the Bay of Smyrna in the summer of 1867, when she was in her twenty-second year. I saw her in the flesh for the first time in New York in the following December. She was slender and beautiful and girlish — and she was both girl and woman. She remained both girl and woman to the last day of her life. Under a grave and gentle exterior burned lasting fires of sympathy, energy, devotion, enthusiasm and absolutely limitless affection. She was always delicate in body and she lived upon her spirit, whose hopefulness and courage were beyond destruction.

She became an invalid at sixteen through falling on the ice and she was never strong again while her life lasted. After that fall she was not able to leave her bed during two years, nor was she able to lie in any position except upon her back. All the great physicians were brought to Elmira one after the other during that time, but there was no helpful result. In those days both worlds were well acquainted with the name of Doctor Newton, a man who was regarded in both worlds as a quack. He moved through the land in state; in majesty, like a king.

One day a relative of the Langdon family came to the house and said; "You have tried everybody else — now try Doctor Newton, the quack. He is downtown at the hotel, practicing upon the wealthy at war prices, and upon the poor for nothing. I saw him wave his hands over Jake Brown's head and take his crutches away from him and send him about his business as good as new. I saw him do the like with others. They may have been hired and there for publicity purposes, and not real. But Jake is genuine. Send for Newton."

Newton came. He found the young girl upon her back. Any attempt to raise her brought sickness and exhaustion and had to be abandoned. Newton opened the windows — long darkened — and delivered a short and fiery prayer; then he put an arm behind her shoulders and said, "Now we will sit up, my child."

The family were alarmed and tried to stop him, but he was not disturbed, and raised her up. She sat several minutes without sickness or discomfort. Then Newton said, "Now we will walk a few steps, my child." He took her out of bed and supported her while she walked several steps; then he said, "I have reached the limit of my art. She is not cured. It is not likely that she will ever be cured. She will never be able to walk far, but after a little daily practice she will be able to walk one or two hundred yards, and she can depend on being able to do that for the rest of her life. "

His charge was fifteen hundred dollars and it was easily worth a hundred thousand. For from that day when she was eighteen until she was fifty- six she was always able to walk a couple of hundred yards with- out stopping to rest; and more than once I saw her walk a quarter of a mile without serious exhaustion.

Crowds gathered around Newton in Dublin, in London and in other places. This happened rather frequently in Europe and in America but the grateful Langdons and Clemenses were never among the crowd. I met Newton once, in after years, and asked him what his secret was. He said he didn't know but thought perhaps some form of electricity proceeded from his body and caused the cures.

Perfect truth and perfect honesty were qualities of my wife's character which were born with her. Her judgments of people and things were sure and without error. Her instincts almost never deceived her. In her judgments of the characters and acts of both friends and strangers there was always room for charity, and this charity never failed. I have compared and contrasted her with hundreds of persons and my feeling remains that hers was the most perfect character I have ever met. And I may add that she had more dignity than any person I have ever known.

She was always cheerful; and she was always able to pass along her cheerfulness to others. During the nine years that we spent in poverty and debt she was always able to reason me out of my despairs and find a bright side to the clouds and make me see it. In all that time I never knew her to utter a word of regret concerning our circumstances, nor did I ever know her children to do the like. For she had taught them and they drew their bravery from her. The love which she gave to those whom she loved took the form of worship, and in that form it was returned.

She had the heart-free laugh of a girl. It came seldom, but when it broke upon the ear it was like music. I heard it for the last time when she had been occupying her sick bed for more than a year and I made a written note of it at the time — a note not to be repeated.

Tomorrow will be the thirty- sixth anniversary. We were married in her father's house in Elmira, New York, and went next day by special train to Buffalo, where I was to be one of the editors of the Buffalo Express and a part owner of the paper. I knew nothing about Buffalo, but I had made my household arrangements through a friend, by letter. I had instructed him to find a boarding house of as respectable a character as my light salary would command. We were received at about nine o'clock at the station in Buffalo and then driven all over America, it seemed to me. I became very angry at that friend for securing a boarding house that apparently had no definite locality. But there was a plot — and my bride knew of it, but I was in the dark. Her father had bought and furnished a new house for us in a fashionable street, and had hired a cook and house-maids and a bright young coachman, an Irishman, Patrick McAleer — and we were being driven all over the city in order that a group of these people would have time to go over to the house and prepare a hot supper. We arrived at last, and when I entered that splendid place my anger reached high-water mark, and without any reserve I delivered my opinion of that friend who was so stupid as to put us in a boarding house whose terms would be far out of reach. Then Mr. Langdon brought for a very pretty box and opened it and took from it a deed of the house. So the joke ended and we sat down to supper.

The company departed about midnight and left us alone in our new quarters. Then Ellen, the cook, came in to get orders for the morning's marketing — and neither of us knew whether beefsteak was sold by the barrel or by the yard. We confessed this fact, and Ellen was full of Irish delight over it. Patrick McAleer, that bright young Irishman, came in to get his orders for next day — and that was our first glimpse of him.

It sounds easy and swift and smooth but that was not the way of it. It did not happen in that comfortable a way. There were three or four proposals of marriage and just as many declinations. I was traveling far and wide giving lectures, but I managed to arrive in Elmira every now and then to renew my pleading. At last help and good for-tune came from a most unexpected quarter. It was one of those cases so frequent in the past centuries, so infrequent in our day — a case where the hand of Providence is in it.

I was ready to leave for New York. A wagon stood outside the main gate of the Langdons' house, with my trunk in it, and Barney, the coachman, was already in the front seat. It was eight or nine in the evening and dark. I said good-by to the grouped family on the front porch, and Charley and I went out and climbed into the wagon. We took our places back of the coachman on the remaining seat, which was toward the end of the wagon and was not fastened in its place; a fact which — most fortunately for me — we were not aware of. Charley was smoking. Barney touched the horse with the whip. He made a sudden spring forward. Charley and I went out over the back of the wagon. In the darkness the red bud of fire on the end of his cigar described a curve through the air which I can see yet. I struck exactly on the top of my head and stood up that way for a moment, then fell down to the earth unconscious. My head just happened to strike a dish formed by four stones which met along the edges. The depression was half full of fresh new sand, for they had been repairing the road. This made a useful pillow. My head did not touch any of those stones. I was not even shaken up. Nothing was the matter with me at all.

Charley was considerably damaged, but in his worry over me he was almost unaware of it. The whole family ran out. It was very pleasant to hear the pitying remarks being made around me. That was one of the happiest half dozen moments of my life. There was nothing to spoil it — except that I had escaped damage. I was afraid that this would be discovered sooner or later. I was such a dead weight that it required the combined strength of Barney and two others to carry me into their house, but it was accomplished. I was there. I recognized that this was victory. I was there.

They set me up in an armchair and sent for the family physician. Poor old creature, it was wrong to get him out but it was business, and I was too unconscious to protest.

When the old doctor arrived he went at the matter in an educated and practical way — that is to say, he started a search for cuts and wounds and swellings and announced that there were none. He said that if I would go to bed and forget my adventure I would be all right in the morning — which was not so. I was not all right in the morning. I didn't intend to be all right and I was far from being all right. But I said I only needed rest and I didn't need that doctor any more.

I got a good three days' stay out of that adventure and it helped a good deal. It pushed my suit forward several steps. The next visit completed the matter and we became engaged conditionally; the condition being that the parents should consent.

In a private talk Mr. Langdon called my attention to something I had already noticed — which was that I was an almost entirely unknown person; that I was from the other side of the continent and that only those people out there would be able to furnish me a character reference — in case I had a character. I gave him some names, and he said I could go away and wait until he could write to those people and get answers.

In due course answers came. I was sent for and we had another private conference. I had referred him to six distinguished men, among them two churchmen (these were all San Franciscans), and he himself had written to a man who worked in a bank who had in earlier years been a Sunday-school superintendent in Elmira and well known to Mr. Langdon. The results were not promising. All those men were frank to a fault. They not only spoke in disapproval of me but they were quite unnecessarily enthusiastic about it. One churchman and that former Sunday-school superintendent added to their black lies the statement that in their belief I would fill a drunkard's grave.

The reading of the letters being finished, there was a good deal of a pause and it consisted largely of sadness and gravity. I couldn't think of anything to say. Mr. Langdon was apparently in the same condition. Finally he raised his handsome head, fixed his clear and honest eye upon me and said, "What kind of people are these? Haven't you a friend in the world?"

I said, "Apparently not."

Then he said, "I'll be your friend myself. Take the girl. I know you better than they do."

Thus happily was my fate settled.

The date of our engagement was February 4, 1869. The engagement ring was plain and of heavy gold. That date was engraved inside of it. A year later I took it from her finger and prepared it to do service as a wedding ring by having the wedding date added and engraved inside of it — February 2, 1870. It was never again removed from her finger for even a moment.

In Italy, when death had restored her vanished youth to her sweet face and she lay fair and beautiful and looking as she had looked when she was a girl and bride, they were going to take that ring from her finger to keep for the children. But I prevented this. It is buried with her.

CHAPTER 24

Our first child, Langdon Clemens, was born the 7th of November, 1870, and lived twenty-two months. I was the cause of the child's illness. His mother trusted him to my care and I took him for a long drive in an open carriage for an airing. It was a raw, cold morning but he was well wrapped about with furs and, in the hands of a careful person, no harm could have come to him. But I soon dropped into a daydream and forgot all about my charge. The furs fell away and left his legs uncovered. By and by the coachman noticed this and I arranged the wraps again, but it was too late. The child was stiff with cold. I hurried home with him. I was horrified at what I had done and I feared the consequences. I have always felt shame for that morning's carelessness and have not allowed myself to think of it when I could help it. I doubt if I had the courage to make confession at that time. I think it most likely that I have never confessed until now.

Susy was born the 19th of March, 1872. The summer seasons of her childhood were spent at Quarry Farm on the hills east of Elmira, New York; the other seasons of the year at the home in Hartford, where we moved in 1871.

Mark Twain's picturesque Home, in Hartford, Connecticut.

Like other children she was gay and happy, fond of play; unlike the average child, she was at times much given to retiring within herself and trying to search out the hidden meanings of the deep things that make the puzzle of human existence. When Susy was aged seven her mother several times said to her, "There, there, Susy, you mustn't cry over little things."

This furnished Susy food for thought. She had been breaking her heart over what had seemed vast tragedy — a broken toy, an outing called off by thunder and lightning and rain, the mouse that was growing tame and friendly in the nursery caught and killed by the cat. (How do you tell the great things from the small ones?) She examined the problem earnestly and long. At last she gave up and went to her mother for help.

"Mamma, what is 'little things'?"

It seemed a simple question — at first. And yet before the answer could be put into words, unsuspected and unexpected difficulties began to appear. They increased; they multiplied. The effort to explain came to a standstill. Then Susy tried to help her mother out — with an instance, an example, an illustration. The mother was getting ready to go downtown, and one of her tasks was to buy a long-promised toy watch for Susy.

"If you forgot the watch, Mamma, would that be a little thing?"

She was not concerned about the watch, for she knew it would not be forgotten. What she was hoping for was that the answer would bring rest and peace to her troubled little mind.

The hope was disappointed, of course — for the reason that the size of bad luck is not determinable by an outsider's measurement of it but only by the measurements applied to it by the person specially affected by it. The king's lost crown is a vast matter to the king but of no consequence to the child. The lost toy is a great matter to the child but in the king's eyes it is not a thing to break the heart about.

As a child Susy had a passionate temper, and it cost her many tears before she learned to govern it; but after that it was a flavorous salt and her character was the stronger and healthier for its presence. It enabled her to be good with dignity; it preserved her not only from being good for pride's sake but from even the appearance of it. In looking back over the long-vanished years it seems but natural and excusable that I should dwell with longing affection and preference upon incidents of her young life that made it beautiful to us, and that I should let its few and small things that offended go unmentioned.

In the summer of 1880, when Susy was just eight years of age, the family were at Quarry Farm, on top of a high hill three miles from Elmira. Haycutting time was coming near and Susy and Clara were counting the hours, for the time was of great importance for them; they had been promised that they might climb on the wagon and ride home from the fields on the top of the mountain of hay. This privilege, so dear to their age and kind, had never been granted them before. They could talk of nothing but this history- making adventure now. But misfortune overtook Susy on the very morning of that important day. In a sudden outbreak of temper she hit Clara with a stick. The offense com- mitted was of a seriousness clearly beyond the limit allowed in the nursery. In accordance with the rule and custom of the house, Susy went to her mother to confess and to help decide upon the size and character of the punishment due. It was quite understood that a punishment could have but one object — to act as a reminder and warn the sinner against sinning in the same way again. Susy and her mother discussed various punishments but none of them seemed sufficient.

This fault was an unusually serious one and required the setting up of a danger signal in the memory that would not blow out nor burn out but remain there and furnish its saving warning indefinitely. Among the punishments mentioned was not being allowed the hay-wagon ride. It was noticeable that this one hit Susy hard. Finally, in the summing up, the mother named over the list and asked, "Which one do you think it ought to be, Susy?"

Susy studied, avoided her duty, and asked, "Which do you think, Mamma?"

"Well, Susy, I would rather leave it to you. You make the choice yourself. "

It cost Susy a struggle and much and deep thinking and weighing — but she came out where anyone who knew her could have known she would:

"Well, Mamma, I'll make it the hay wagon, because, you know, the other things might not make me remember not to do it again, but if I don't get the ride on the hay wagon I can remember it easily."

In this world the real penalty, the sharp one, the lasting one, never falls otherwise than on the wrong person. It was not I that hit Clara but the remembrance of poor Susy's lost hay ride still brings me a feeling as though I had been punished after twenty-six years.

CHAPTER 25

When Susy was thirteen and a slender little maid with copper-brown hair down her back and was perhaps the busiest person in the household, by reason of the many studies, health exercises and pleasures she had to attend to, she secretly and of her own motion and out of love added another task to her labors — the writing of a biography of me. She did this work in her bedroom at night and kept her record hidden. After a little, the mother discovered it and took it and let me see it; then told Susy what she had done and how pleased I was and how proud. I remember that time with a deep pleasure. I had had praise before but none that touched me like this; none that could approach it for value in my eyes. It has kept that place always since. As I read it now, after all these many years, it is still a king's message to me and brings me the same dear surprise it brought me then — with the sadness added of the thought that the eager and hasty hand that wrote it will never touch mine again — and I feel as the humble and unexpectant must feel when their eyes fall upon the paper that raises them to the ranks of the noble.

I cannot bring myself to change any line or word in Susy's picture of me but will introduce passages from it just as they came in their simplicity out of her honest heart, which was the beautiful heart of a child. What comes from that source has a charm and grace of its own which may break all the recognized laws of literature, if it choose, and yet be literature still.

The spelling is frequently desperate but it was Susy's and it shall stand. I love it and to me it is gold. To correct it would mix it with impurities rather than refine it. It would spoil it. It would take from it its freedom and make it stiff and stylish. It is Susy's spelling and she was doing the best she could — and nothing could better it for me.

She learned languages easily; she learned history easily; she learned music easily; she learned all things easily, quickly and thoroughly except spelling. She even learned that after a while. But it would have grieved me but little if she had failed in it — for although good spelling was my one accomplishment I was never able to greatly respect it. That is my feeling yet. Before the spelling-book came with its rules and forms, men unconsciously revealed shades of their characters and also added en- lightening shades of expression to what they wrote by their spelling, and so it is possible that the spelling-book has been of doubtful value to us.

Susy began the biography in 1885, when I was in the fiftieth year of my age, and she in the fourteenth of hers. She begins in this way:

We are a very happy family. We consist of Papa, Mamma, Jean, Clara and me. It is papa I am writing about, and I shall have no trouble in not knowing what to say about him, as he is a very striking character.

Papa's appearance has been described many times, but very incorrectly. He had beautiful gray hair, not any too thick or too long, but just right; a Roman nose, which greatly improves the beauty of his features; kind blue eyes and a small mustache. He had a wonderfully shaped head and a very good figure — in short, he is an extrodinarily fine looking man. His skin is very fair, and he doesn't ware a beard. He is a very good man and a very funny man. He has got a temper, but we all of us have in this family. He is the loveliest man I ever saw or ever hope to see — and oh, so absent-minded. He does tell perfectly delightful stories....

Papa has a peculiar way of walking, it seems just to sute him, but most people do not; he always walks up and down the room while thinking and between each coarse at meals....

Papa uses very strong language, but I have an idea not nearly so strong as when he first maried Mamma. A lady acquaintance of his is rather likely to interupt what one is saying, and papa told mamma that he thought he should say to the lady's husband "I am glad your wife wasn't present when God said Let there be light."

It is as I have said before. This is a frank historian. She doesn't cover up one's faults but gives them an equal showing with one's handsomer qualities. Of course I made the remark which she has quoted — and even at this distant day I am still as much as half persuaded that if that lady mentioned had been present when the Creator said "Let there be light" she would have interrupted him and we shouldn't ever have got it.

CHAPTER 26

There is one great trouble about writing an autobiography and that is the numerous and varying ideas that offer themselves when you sit down and are ready to begin. Sometimes the ideas come flooding from twenty directions at once and for a time you are almost drowned. You can use them only one at a time and you don't know which one to choose out of the twenty — still you must choose; there is no help for it; and you choose with the understanding that the nineteen left over are probably left over for good and lost, since they may never suggest themselves again. But this time the words are forced upon me. This is mainly because it is the latest idea that has suggested itself in the last quarter of an hour, and therefore the warmest one, because it has not yet had a chance to cool off. It is a couple of amateur literary offerings. From old experience I know that amateur productions, outwardly offered for one's honest cold judgment, to be followed by an uncolored and honest opinion, are not really offered in that spirit at all. The thing really wanted and expected is praise. Also, my experience has taught me that in almost all amateur cases praise is impossible — if it is to be backed by honesty.

I have this moment finished reading this morning's pair of offerings and am a little troubled. If they had come from strangers, I should not have given myself the pain of reading them, but should have returned them unread, according to my custom, pleading that I lack an editor's training and therefore am not qualified to sit in judgment upon anyone's literature but my own. But this morning's harvest came from friends and that alters the case. I have read them and the result is as usual: they are not literature. They do contain meat but the meat is only half cooked. The meat is certainly there and if it could pass through the hands of an expert cook the result would be a very satisfactory dish indeed. One of this morning's works does really come near to being literature, but the amateur's hand is exposed with a fatal frequency and the exposure spoils it. The author's idea is, in case I shall render a favorable opinion, to offer the story to a magazine.

There is something about this childlike daring that compels admiration. It is a reckless daring which I suppose is exhibited in no field but one — the field of literature. We see something approaching it in war, but approaching it only distantly. The untrained common soldier has often offered himself in a hopeless cause and stood cheerfully ready to encounter all its dangers — but we draw the line there. Not even the most confident untrained soldier offers himself as a candidate for a generalship, yet this is what the amateur author does. With his un- trained pen he puts together his unskilled efforts and offers them to all the magazines, one after the other — that is to say, he proposes them for posts limited to literary generals who have earned their rank and place by years and years of hard and honest training in the lower grades of the service.

I am sure that this happens in no other trade but ours. A person untrained to shoemaking does not offer his services as a shoemaker to the man in charge of a shop — not even the rawest literary hopeful would be so unintelligent as to do that. He would see the humor of it; he would recognize as the most commonplace of facts that an apprentice- ship is necessary in order to qualify a person to be a tinner, bricklayer, printer, horse -doctor, butcher — and any and every other occupation whereby a human being acquires bread and fame. But when it comes to doing literature, his wisdoms vanish all of a sudden and he thinks he finds himself now in the presence of a profession which requires no apprenticeship, no experience, no training — nothing whatsoever but conscious talent and a lion's courage.

We do not realize how strange and curious a thing this is until we look around for an object lesson whereby to realize it to us. We must imagine a similar case — someone who is ambitious for operatic distinction and cash, for instance. He applies to the management for a place as second tenor. The management accepts him, arranges the terms and puts him on the payroll. Understand, this is an imaginary case; I am not pretending that it has happened. Let us proceed.

After the first act the manager calls the second tenor to account and wants to know. He says:

"Have you ever studied music?"

"A little — yes, by myself, at odd times, for amusement." "You have never gone into regular and laborious training, then, for the opera, under the masters of the art?" "No."

"Then what makes you think you could do second tenor in Lohengrin?"

"I thought I could. I wanted to try. I seemed to have a voice."

"Yes, you have a voice, and with five years of hard training under a skilled master you could be successful, perhaps, but I assure you you are not ready for second tenor yet. You have a voice; you have a presence; you have a noble and childlike confidence; you have courage that is immense. These are all essentials and they are in your favor but there are other essentials in this great trade which you still lack. If you can't afford the time and labor necessary to acquire them, leave opera alone and try something which does not require training and experience. Go away now and try for a job in surgery."

We have lived in a Florentine villa before we came here to the

Villa di Quarto. [Editor's note: written in 1904.] This was twelve years ago. This was the Villa Viviani and was pleasantly and commandingly located on a hill overlooking Florence and the great valley. The year spent in the Villa Viviani was something of a contrast to the five months which we have now spent in the Villa di Quarto. Among my old notebooks I find some account of that pleasantly remembered year and will introduce a few of them here.

When we were passing through Florence in the spring of 1892 on our way to Germany, the diseased-world's bathhouse, we began making arrangements for a villa, and friends of ours completed them after we were gone. When we got back three or four months later everything was ready, even to the servants and the dinner. It takes but a sentence to state that, but it makes a lazy person tired to think of the planning and work and trouble that lie concealed in it. For it is less trouble and more satisfaction to bury two families than to select and equip a home for one.

The situation of the villa was perfect. It was three miles from Florence, on the side of a hill. It looked down upon olive trees and vineyards; to the right, beyond some hills, was Fiesole; nearby was the impressive mass of the Ross castle, its walls and towers rich with the weather stains of forgotten centuries; in the distant plain lay Florence, pink and gray and brown, with the high dome of the cathedral ruling over its center, and the right by the smaller dome of the Palazzo Vecchio; all around was the ring of high hills, snowed white with countless villas. After nine months of familiarity with this view I still think, as I thought in the beginning, that this is the fairest picture on our planet, the most wonderful to look upon, the most satisfying to the eye and the spirit.

September 26, 1892. Arrived in Florence. Got my head shaved. This was a mistake. Moved to the villa in the afternoon, some of the trunks brought up in the evening by the "contadino" — if that is his title. He is the man who lives on the farm and takes care of it for the owner. The contadino is middle-aged and like the rest of the farmers — that is to say, brown, handsome, good-natured, courteous and entirely independent without making any offensive show of it. He charged too much for the trunks, I was told. My informant explained that this was customary.

September 27. The rest of the trunks brought up this morning. He charged too much again but I was told that this was also customary. It is all right, then. I do not wish to do violence to the customs. Hired carriage, horses and a coachman. The carriage has seen better days and weighs thirty tons. The horses are weak and object to the carriage; they stop and turn around every now and then and examine it with surprise and suspicion. This causes delay. But it entertains the people along the road. They came out and stood around with their hands in their pockets and discussed the matter with one another. I was told they said that a forty-ton carriage was not the thing for horses like these — what they needed was a cart.

The villa is a two-story house. It is not an old house — from an Italian standpoint, I mean. No doubt there has always been a nice dwelling on this spot since a thousand years B.C., but this present one is said to be only two hundred years old. Outside, it is a plain square building like a box and is painted a light yellow. The garden about the house is stocked with flowers and lemon bushes in great stone containers; there are several tall trees — stately pines — also trees of kinds not familiar to me; roses overflow the retaining walls.

The house is like a fort for strength. The main walls — of brick — are about three feet thick; the walls of the rooms, also of brick, are nearly the same thickness. The ceilings of the rooms on the ground floor are more than twenty feet high; those of the upper floors are also higher than necessary. I have several times tried to count the rooms in the house but the lack of regularity puzzles me. There seem to be twenty-eight.

The curious feature of the house is the salon. This is a big empty space which occupies the center of the house; all the rest of the house is built around it; it extends up through both stories and the sense of its vastness strikes you the moment you step into it and cast your eyes around and up. There are five couches distributed along its walls; they make little or no show, though their length all together is fifty- seven feet. A piano in it is a lost object. We have tried to reduce the sense of desert space and emptiness with tables and things but they have a defeated look and do not do any good. Whatever stands or moves under that high ceiling is dwarfed.

But I am forgetting to state what it is about that room that is so curious — which is, that it is not really vast but only seems so. It is deceiving. Measured by the eye it is sixty feet square and sixty high: but I have been using the measuring line and find it to be but forty feet square and forty high. These are the correct figures; and what is interestingly strange is that the place continues to look as big now as it did before I measured it.

The villa has a roomy look, a spacious look; and when the sun- shine is pouring in and lighting up the bright colors of the shiny floors and walls and ceilings there is a large and friendly suggestion of welcome, but I do not know that I have ever seen a continental dwelling which quite met the American standard of a home in all the details. There is a trick about the American house that is like the deep -lying untranslatable expressions of a foreign language — a trick uncatchable by the stranger, and indescribable; and that trick, that indescribable something, whatever it is, is just the something that gives the home -look and the home -feeling to an American house and makes it the most satisfying shelter yet invented by men — and women — particularly women. The American house is rich in soft and varied colors that please and rest the eye, and in surfaces that are smooth and pleasant to the touch, in forms that are shapely and graceful, in objects without number which compel interest and cover nakedness; and the night has even a higher charm than the day, there, for the lights do really give light instead of merely trying and failing; and under their veiled and colored glow all the comfort and charm of the place is at best and loveliest. But when night shuts down on the continental home there is no gas or electricity to fight it, but only ugly lamps of incomparable poverty in the matter of effectiveness.

September 29. I seem able to forget everything except that I have had my head shaved. The main difficulty is the flies. They like it up there better than anywhere else; on account of the view, I suppose. It seems to me that I have never seen any flies before that had shoes like these. They walk over my head all the time and cause me torture. It is their park, their club, their summer resort. They have garden parties there and all sorts of wild doings. And they fear nothing. All flies are daring but these are more daring than those of other nationalities. These cannot be scared away by any device.

October 1. Finding that the coachman was taking his meals in the kitchen, I reorganized the contract to include his board, at thirty francs a month. That is what it would cost him up above us in the village and I think I can feed him for two hundred and save thirty out of it. Saving thirty is better than not saving anything.

October 6. I find myself at a disadvantage here. Four persons in the house speak Italian and nothing else, one person speaks German and nothing else, the rest of the talk is in the French, English and improper languages. I am equipped with but the merest bit of skill in these tongues, if I except one or two. Angelo speaks French — a French he invented himself; a French which no one can understand. He prefers it to his native Italian. He loves to talk it; loves to listen to himself; to him it is music; he will not let it alone. It makes no difference what language he is addressed in, his reply is in French, his peculiar French, which sounds like pushing coal down a slide. I know a few Italian words and several phrases, and along at first I used to keep them bright and fresh by sharpening them on Angelo; but he partly couldn't understand them and partly didn't want to, so I have been obliged to remove them from the market for the present. But this is not permanent. I am practicing. I am preparing. Some day I shall be ready for him, and not in French but in his native tongue.

October 27. The first month is finished. We agree that life at a Florentine villa is an ideal existence. The weather is divine, the out- side aspects lovely, the days and nights restful; being away from the rest of the world is as restful and satisfactory as a dream. There is no house-keeping to do, no plans to make, no marketing to watch over — all these things do themselves, apparently. One is aware that somebody is attending to them, just as one is aware that the world is being turned over and the sun moved around according to plan, but that is all; one does not feel personally concerned or in any way responsible. Yet there is no head, no chief boss; each servant minds his or her own department, requiring no watching over and having none. There is no noise or quarreling or confusion — upstairs. I don't know what goes on below. Late in the afternoons friends come out from the city and drink tea in the open air and tell what is happening in the world; and when the great sun sinks down upon Florence and the daily wonder begins, they hold their breaths and look. It is not a time for talk.

CHAPTER 28

Susy passed from life in the Hartford home the 18th of August, 1896. With her when the end came were Jean and Katy Leary and the gardener and his wife. Clara and her mother and I arrived in England from around the world on the 31st of July and took a house in Guildford. A week later, when Susy, Katy and Jean should have been arriving from America, we got a letter instead.

It explained that Susy was slightly ill — nothing to worry about. But we were uneasy and began to cable for later news. This was Friday. All day no answer — and the ship to leave Southampton next day at noon. Clara and her mother began packing, to be ready in case the news should be bad. Finally came a cable saying, "Wait for cable in the morning." This was not satisfactory — not reassuring. I cabled again, asking that the answer be sent to Southampton, for the day was now closing. We sat silent at home till one in the morning, waiting — waiting for we knew not what. Then we took the earliest morning train and when we reached Southampton the message was there. It said the recovery would be long but certain. This was a great relief to me but not to my wife. She was frightened. She and Clara went aboard ship at once and sailed for America to nurse Susy. I remained behind to search for another and large house in Guildford.

That was the 15th of August, 1896. Three days later, when my wife and Clara were about halfway across the ocean, I was standing in our dining room, thinking of nothing in particular, when a cable was put into my hand. It said, "Susy was peacefully released today."

It is one of the mysteries of our nature that a man, all unprepared, can receive a thunderstroke like that and live. There is but one reason- able explanation of it. The mind is knocked out by the shock and barely gathers the meaning of the words. The power to realize their full import is mercifully wanting. The mind has a dumb sense of vast loss — that is all. It will take mind and memory months and possibly years to gather together the details and thus learn and know the whole extent of the loss.

The 18th of August brought me the awful news. The mother and the sister were out there in mid- Atlantic, ignorant of what was hap- pening, flying to meet this dreadful event. All that could be done to protect them from the full force of the shock was done by relatives and good friends. They went down the Bay and met the ship at night but did not show themselves until morning, and then only to Clara. When she returned to the stateroom she did not speak and did not need to. Her mother looked at her and said, "Susy is dead."

At half past ten o'clock that night Clara and her mother completed their circle of the globe and drew up at Elmira by the same train and in the same car which had taken them and me westward from it one year, one month, and one week before. And again Susy was there — not waving her welcome as she had waved her farewell to us thirteen months before, but lying white and fair in her coffin in the house where she was born.

The last thirteen days of Susy's life were spent in our own house in Hartford, the home of her childhood and always the dearest place on earth to her. About her she had faithful old friends; her uncle and aunt; Patrick, the coachman; Katy, who had begun to serve us when Susy was a child of eight; John and Ellen, who had been with us many years. Also, Jean was there.

At the hour when my wife and Clara set sail for America, Susy was in no danger. Three hours later there came a sudden change for the worse. Meningitis set in and it was immediately apparent that she was death-struck. That was Saturday, the 15th of August.

"That evening she took food for the last time. (Jean's letter to me.) The next morning the brain fever was raging. She walked the floor a little in her pain and high fever, then grew very weak and returned to her bed. Previously she had found hanging in a closet a gown which she had seen her mother wear. She thought it was her mother, dead, and she kissed it and cried. About noon she became blind (an effect of the disease). About one in the afternoon Susy spoke for the last time."

It was only one word that she said when she spoke that last time and it told of her longing. She felt with her hands and found Katy and stroked her face and said, "Mamma."

About two o'clock she composed herself as if for sleep and never moved again. She fell into unconsciousness and so remained two days and five hours, until Tuesday evening at seven minutes past seven, when the release came. She was twenty-four years and five months old.

On the 23rd her mother and her sisters saw her laid to rest — she that had been our wonder and our worship.

CHAPTER 29

Tomorrow will be the 5th of June (1906), a day which marks the tragedy of my life — the death of my wife. It occurred two years ago, in Florence, Italy, where we had taken her in the hope of restoring her broken health.

The writing of this autobiography, which was begun in Florence in the beginning of 1904, was soon interrupted because of the anxious times, and I was never moved to resume the work until January, 1906, for I did not see how I was ever going to bring myself to speak in detail of the mournful and lonely experiences of that sad interval and of the twenty-two months of wearing distress which came before it.

Mrs. Clemens had never been strong, and a thirteen months' jour- ney around the world seemed a doubtful experiment for her, but it turned out to be a safe one. Her health seemed improved, although there was burning summer heat in Australia, New Zealand, and Tasmania. It was still summer when we sailed from Melbourne on the 1st of January, '96. It was very hot in Ceylon, of course, as it always is. It was still summer to us all over India until the 17th of March, when an English physician in Jeypore told us to hurry to Calcutta and get out of India immediately, because the warm weather could come at any time now and it would be perilous for us. So we suffered through the "cold weather," as they called it there, clear from Rawal Pindi to Calcutta, and took ship for South Africa — and still Mrs. Clemens's health had steadily improved. She and Clara went with me all over my lecture course in South Africa, except to Pretoria, and she never had a day's illness.

We finally finished our lecture expedition on the 14th of July, '96, sailed for England the next day and landed at Southampton on the 31st. Two weeks later Mrs. Clemens and Clara sailed for home to nurse Susy through a reported illness and found her in her coffin in her grandmother's house.

The now smaller family presently joined me in England. We lived in London, in Switzerland, in Vienna, in Sweden, and again in London, until October, 1900. And when at that time we took ship, bound for home, Mrs. Clemens's health and strength were in better condition than they had ever been since she was sixteen years old and met with the accident which I have before mentioned.

We took a house in New York, just off Fifth Avenue, for a year, and there the overtaxing of Mrs. Clemens's strength began. The house was large; housekeeping was a heavy labor — as indeed it always is in New York. Social life was another heavy tax upon her strength. In the drive and rush of the midwinter New York season my correspondence grew beyond my secretary's strength and mine, and I found that Mrs. Clemens was trying to ease the burden for us. One day I wrote thirty-two brief letters with my own hand, and then found, to my horror, that Mrs. Clemens had written the same number. She had added this labor to her other labors and they were already too heavy for her.

By the following June this kind of life, after her nine and a half years of peaceful and effortless life in Europe, began to exhibit effects. Three months' rest in the Adirondacks did her a great deal of good. Then we took a house in Riverdale-on-the - Hudson. It was a large house, and again the housekeeping burden was heavy. Early in 1902 she was threatened with a nervous breakdown, but soon the danger seemed past.

At the end of June we secured a furnished home near York Harbor for the summer. We went sailing in the lovely weather on Mr. Rogers's fast steam yacht. But she could not rest. She was never intended to rest.

She had the spirit of a steam engine in a frame of flesh. It was always taxing that frame with its tireless energy; it was always exacting of it labors that were beyond its strength. Soon her heart began to alarm her. Her alarm increased rapidly. Within two weeks she began to dread driving out. This was the condition of things all through July.

At seven on the morning of August the eleventh I was awakened by a cry. I saw Mrs. Clemens standing on the opposite side of the room, leaning against the wall for support, and gasping. She said, "I am dying."

I helped her back to the bed and sent for Doctor Leonard, a New York physician. He said it was a nervous breakdown and that nothing but absolute rest, staying alone, and careful nursing could help her. That was the beginning. During the next twenty-two months she had for society physicians and trained nurses only, broadly speaking.

The next sixty days were anxious ones for us. Clara stood a daily watch of three or four hours, and hers was a hard office indeed. Daily she sealed up in her heart a dozen dangerous truths and thus saved her mother's life and hope and happiness with holy lies. She had never told her mother a lie in her life before, and I may almost say that she never told her a truth afterward. It was fortunate for all of us that Clara's reputation for truthfulness was so well established in her mother's mind. It was our daily protection from tragedy. I was never able to get a reputation like Clara's. It would have been useful to me now, but it was too late to begin the labor of securing it, and I furnished no information in the bedroom. But my protection lay in the fact that I was allowed in the bedroom only once a day, then for only two minutes. The nurse stood at the door with her watch in her hand and turned me out when the time was up.

Toward the end of October (1902) we took Mrs. Clemens to Italy with her nurse. We took our patient to the Villa di Quarto. She had been ill many times in her life but her marvelous powers of recovery always brought her out of these perils safely. We were full of fears all the time but I do not think we ever really lost hope. At least not until the last two or three weeks. It was not like her to lose hope. We never expected her to lose it — and so at last when she looked me in the eyes and said, "You believe I shall get well?" it was a form which she had never used before and it was a betrayal. Her hope was perishing, and I recognized it.

CHAPTER 30

Sunday Evening, June 5, 1904 — 11:15 o'clock. She has been dead two hours. It is impossible. The words have no meaning. But they are true; I know it, without realizing it. She was my life and she is gone.

Only four hours ago I sat by her bedside while Clara and Jean were at dinner and she was bright and cheerful — a rare thing these last miserable weeks — and she would talk, although it was a forbidden privilege, because she was so easily tired. She was full of interest in the calls which Jean and I had been making, and asked all about the people, and was like her old self. And smiled! Just her natural smile. It was like sunshine breaking through weeks of cloud. It lifted me up and made me believe the impossible — that she would walk again, be our comrade again. Poor tired child, how she loved her life, how lovingly and eagerly she held fast to it through all these twenty-two months of confinement and loneliness and bodily suffering.

I was deceived by her spirit and liveliness, and far overstayed my visit. Then I blamed myself and said I had done wrong; but she said there was no harm. "You will come back?" and I said, "Yes, to say good night" — meaning at half-past nine, as usual these many months.

For a time I sat in my room, filled with a deep contentment, my heart-burdens strangely gone, my spirit at peace for the first time in so many heavy months. Then I did a thing which I have hardly done since we lost our incomparable Susy eight years ago — I went to the piano and sang the old songs, the Negro hymns no one cared for when I sang them, except Susy and her mother. After a little I went to my room, and it was now getting toward time to go downstairs and say good night; for it was a quarter past nine, and I must not go later than half past. At that moment Livy was breathing her last.

At the head of the stairs I met the nurse, who had come for me. I thought nothing of that; I merely supposed that Livy was tired and ought to be quieting down for the night.

Livy was sitting up in bed, with her head bent forward — she had not been able to lie down for seven months — and Katy was on one side of the bed and the nurse on the other, supporting her; Clara and Jean were standing near the foot of the bed, looking in a state of shock. I went around and bent over and looked into Livy's face, and I think that I spoke to her, I do not know; but she did not speak to me and that seemed strange. I could not understand it. I kept looking at her and wondering — and never dreamed of what had happened! Then Clara said, "But is it true? Katy, is it true? It can't be true!" Katy burst into sobbings, and then for the first time I knew.

It was twenty minutes past nine. Only five minutes before, she had been speaking. She had heard me at the piano and had said to the nurse, "He is singing a good-night song for me. " They had no idea that she was near to death. She was happy and was speaking — and in an instant she was gone from this life. Five times in the last four months she spent an hour and more fighting violently for breath, and she lived in the awful fear of choking to death. Mercifully she was granted the gentlest and swiftest of deaths — by heart failure — and she never knew, she never knew!

She was the most beautiful spirit, and the highest and the noblest I have known. And now she is dead.

CHAPTER 31

A FEW DAYS AGO I WROTE JOHN HOWELLS SOME STRONG PRAISES of his work as a designer of this house. I remember John as a little child, and it seems strange and impossible that I have lived, and lived, and lived, and gone on continuously living, until at last that child, chasing along in my wake, has built a house for me and put a roof over my head. I can't realize that this is that child.

Speaking of youth, I am reminded that with some frequency people say to me, "You wouldn't look so young if you had the bald head proper to your time of life; how do you preserve that crop of hair?" I have to answer them with a theory, for lack of real knowledge. I tell them I think my hair remains with me because I keep it clean; keep it clean by thoroughly washing it with soap and water every morning, then rinsing it well; then soaping it heavily and rubbing off the soap with a coarse cloth, a process which leaves a slight coating of oil upon each hair — oil from the soap. The cleansing and the oiling combined leave the hair soft and silky, and pleasantly and comfortably wearable the whole day through; for although the hair becomes dirty again with- in ten hours, either in country or city, it does not become dirty enough to be really rough to the touch and delicately uncomfortable under twenty- four hours; yet it does become dirty enough in twenty-four hours to make the water cloudy when I wash it.

Now we arrive at a curious thing; the answer to my explanation always brings forth the same old unvarying and foolish remark, to wit — "Water ruins the hair because it causes the roots to become rotten." This remark is not made in a doubtful tone but in a decided one. Then I say, "How do you know this?" and the confident speaker stands exposed; he doesn't know what to say. If I ask him if he has ruined his own hair by wetting it, it turns out that he doesn't wet it often, there- fore he is not speaking from experience; if I ask him if he has personal knowledge of cases where the roots turned rotten because of wetting, it turns out he hasn't a single case of the kind to offer.

Strange — it is just like religion and politics! In religion and politics people's beliefs are in almost every case gotten at second-hand, and without examination, from authorities who have not themselves examined the questions at issue but have taken them at second-hand from other nonexaminers, whose opinions about them are not worth one cent.

The human race is odd and curious and interesting. It is constantly washing its face, its eyes, its ears, its nose, its teeth, its mouth, its feet, its legs, and it is thoroughly convinced that cleanliness is next to godliness, and that water is the noblest and surest of all preservers of health, and wholly undangerous, except in just one case — you mustn't apply it to your hair!

The more one examines this matter the more curious it becomes. Every man wets and soaps his hands before he goes to dinner; he washes them before supper; he washes them before breakfast; he washes them before lunch, and he knows, not by guesswork, but by experience, that in all these cases his hands are dirty and need the washing when he applies it. Does he suppose that his bare and unprotected hair, exposed exactly as his hands are exposed, is not gathering dirt all the time?

I am considered peculiar because I wear white clothes both winter and summer. I am peculiar, then, because I prefer to be clean in the matter of clothing — clean in a dirty world; absolutely the only cleanly clothed human being in all Christendom north of the tropics. And that is what I am. All clothing gets dirty in a single day — as dirty as one's hands would get in that length of time if one washed them only once; a neglect which any lady or gentleman would scorn to be guilty of. All the Christian world wears dark-colored clothes; after the first day's wear they are dirty, and they continue to get dirtier and dirtier, day after day, and week after week, to the end of their service. Men look fine in their black dress clothes at a fancy dinner, but often those dress-suits are rather real estate than personal property; they carry so much soil that you could plant seeds in them and raise a crop.

CHAPTER 32

Stormfield, Christmas Eve
11 a.m., 1909

Jean is dead.

Has anyone ever tried to put upon paper all the little happenings connected with a dear one — happenings of the twenty-four hours coming before the sudden and unexpected death of that dear one? Would a book contain them? Would two books contain them? I think not. They pour into the mind in a flood. They are little things that have always been happening every day, and were so unimportant and easily forgettable before — but now! Now how different! How precious they are, how dear, how unforgettable!

Last night Jean, full of splendid health, and I the same, from the effects of my Bermuda holiday, walked hand in hand from the dinner table and sat down in the library and talked and planned and discussed, cheerily and happily (and how unsuspectingly) until nine — which is late for us — then went upstairs. At my door Jean said, "I can't kiss you good night, Father: I have a cold and you could catch it." I bent and Jean Clemens died early in the morning of December 24, 1909. Two days later Mark Twain showed the following account to Albert Bigelow Paine (his friend and biographer) and said, "If you think it worthy, some day — at the proper time it can end my autobiography.

Mark Twain's daughter, Jean Clemens (picture was taken pre 1909).

It is the final chapter." He died four months later, on April 21, 1910...

I bent and kissed her hand. She was moved — I saw it in her eyes — and she impulsively kissed my hand in return. Then with the usual gay "Sleep well, dear!" from us both, we parted.

At half-past seven this morning I woke and heard voices outside my door. I said to myself, "Jean is starting on her usual horseback flight to the station for the mail." Then Katy, who had been in the service of our family for twenty-nine years, entered, stood shaking and gasping at my bedside a moment, then found her tongue:

"Miss Jean is dead!"

Possibly I know now what the soldier feels when a shot is fired through his heart.

In her bathroom there she lay, the fair young creature, stretched upon the floor and covered with a sheet. And looking so peaceful, so natural, and as if asleep. We knew what had happened. She was an epileptic: she had been seized with a fit and heart failure in her bath. The doctor had to come several miles. His efforts, like our own previous ones, failed to bring her back to life.

Four days ago I came back from a months holiday in Bermuda in perfected health; but by some accident the reporters failed to perceive this. Day before yesterday, letters and telegrams began to arrive from friends and strangers which indicated that I was supposed to be dangerously ill. Yesterday Jean begged me to explain my case through the newspaper wire services. I said it was not important enough; but she was distressed and said I must think of Clara. Clara would see the report in the German papers, and as she had been nursing her husband day and night for four months and was worn out the shock might be dangerous.

Mark Twain, standing, facing right, wearing cap and gown, with 5 other people at the wedding of Clara Clemens (picture taken in 1835-1910).

There was reason in that; so I sent a humorous paragraph by telephone to the wire service denying the "charge" that I was "dying" and saying, "I would not do such a thing at my time of life."

Jean was a little troubled and did not like to see me treat the matter so lightly! but I said it was best to treat it so, for there was nothing serious about it. This morning I sent the sorrowful facts of this day's tragedy to the wire service. Will both appear in the evening's papers? — the one so light, the other so sad.

I lost Susy thirteen years ago; I lost her mother — her incomparable mother! five and a half years ago; Clara has gone away to live in Europe; and now I have lost Jean. How poor I am, who was once so rich!

Seventy-four years old, twenty-four days ago. Seventy-four years old yesterday. Who can estimate my age today?

I have looked upon her again. I wonder I can bear it. She looks just as her mother looked when she lay dead in Florence so long ago. Death is more beautiful than sleep.

I saw her mother buried. I said I would never endure that horror again; that I would never again look into the grave of anyone dear to me. I have kept to that. They will take Jean from this house tomorrow and bear her to Elmira, New York, where lie those of us that have been released, but I shall not follow.

Jean was there when my ship came in only four days ago. She was at the door, smiling a welcome, when I reached this house the next evening. We played cards and she tried to teach me a new game called "Mark Twain." She wouldn't let me look into the next room, where she was making Christmas preparations. She said she would finish them in the morning. While she was out for a moment I stole a look. The uncompleted surprise was there: in the form of a Christmas tree decorated with silver in a most wonderful way; and on a table were the many bright things which she was going to hang upon it today.

All these little things happened such a few hours ago — and now she lies dead, and cares for nothing any more. Strange — marvelous — unbelievable. I have had this experience before, but it would still be unbelievable if I had had it a thousand times.

"Miss Jean is dead!"

That is what Katy said. When I heard the door open behind the bed I supposed it was Jean coming to kiss me good morning....

I have been to Jean's room. Such a lot of Christmas presents for servants and friends! They are everywhere; tables, chairs, the floor — everything is occupied and over-occupied. It is many and many a year since I have seen the like. In that ancient day Mrs. Clemens and I used to slip softly into the nursery at midnight on Christmas Eve and look the display of presents over. The children were little then. And now here is Jean's room looking just as that nursery used to look. The presents are not yet marked — the hands are forever idle that would have marked them today. Jean's mother always worked herself down with her Christmas preparations. Jean did the same yesterday and the days before, and the tiredness may have cost her life.

In the talk last night I said I found everything going so smoothly that if she were willing I would go back to Bermuda in February again for another month. She was anxious that I should do it, and said that if I would put off the trip until March she would take Katy and go with me. We shook hands upon that and said it was settled. I had a mind to write to Bermuda by tomorrow's ship and secure a furnished house and servants. I meant to write the letter this morning. But it will never be written now.

Why did I build this house, two years ago? To shelter this vast emptiness? How foolish I was. But I shall stay in it. The spirits of the dead bless a house for me. It was not so with other members of my family. Susy died in the house we built in Hartford. Mrs. Clemens would never enter it again. But it made the house dearer to me. I have entered it once since, when it was empty and silent, but to me it was a holy place and beautiful. It seemed to me that the spirits of the dead were all about me and would speak to me and welcome me if they could. Clara and Jean would never enter the New York hotel which their mother had frequented in earlier days. They could not bear it. But I shall stay in this house. It is dearer to me tonight than ever it was before. Jean's spirit will make it beautiful for me always. Her lonely and tragic death — but I will not think of that now.

There was never a kinder heart than Jean's. From her childhood up she always spent the most of her allowance on charities of one kind and another. After she had her income doubled she spent her money upon these things with a free hand.

She was a faithful friend to all animals and she loved them all, birds, beasts and everything — even snakes — this she acquired from me.

She knew all the birds. She founded two or three societies for the protection of animals, here and in Europe.

She thought all letters deserved the civility of an answer. Her mother brought her up in that kindly error. She could write a good letter and was swift with her pen. She had but an indifferent ear for music, but her tongue took to languages with ease. She never allowed her Italian, French and German to become neglected.

Christmas Day. Noon. Last night I went to Jean's room several times and turned back the sheet and looked at the peaceful face and kissed the cold brow and remembered that heart-breaking night in Florence so long ago, in that silent vast villa, when I crept downstairs so many times and turned back a sheet and looked at a face just like this one — Jean's mother's face — and kissed a brow that was just like this one. And last night I saw again what I had seen then — that strange and lovely thing — the sweet, soft face of early maidenhood restored by the gracious hand of death.

Christmas Night. This afternoon they took her away from her room. As soon as I might, I went down to the library and there she lay in her coffin dressed in exactly the same clothes she wore when she stood at the other end of the room on the sixth of October last, as Clara's chief bridesmaid. Her face was glowing with happy excitement then; it was the same face now, with the dignity of death and the peace of God upon it.

December 26. 2:30 p.m. It is the time appointed. The funeral has begun. Four hundred miles away, but I can see it all just as if I were there. The scene is the library in the Langdon home. Jean's coffin stands where her mother and I stood, forty years ago, and were married; and where Susy's coffin stood thirteen years ago; where her mother's stood five and a half ago; and where mine will stand, after a little time.

Five o'clock. It is all over.

When Clara went away two weeks ago to live in Europe, it was hard but I could bear it, for I had Jean left. I said we would be a family. We said we would be close comrades and happy — just we two. That fair dream was in my mind when Jean met me at the ship last Monday; it was in my mind when she received me at the door last Tuesday evening. We were together; we were a family! the dream had come true — oh, preciously true, contentedly true, satisfying true! and remained true two whole days.

And now? Now Jean is in her grave!

In the grave — if I can believe it. God rest her sweet spirit!

GLOSSARY

amateur: One who practices an art for the love of it; not a professional,
anniversary: A day separated by a year or an exact number of years
from some past event.

apprentice: A beginner who is learning a trade; usually not a paid
worker.

autobiography: One's life story or history written by himself,
bald: Without hair,
biography: A life story.

board, boarding house: Meals at a fixed price, usually at a house in
which one also has a room.

cathedral: The chief church which is the seat of the head of that religious group in a certain region,
celebrated: famous, widely known,
coarse: Susy's misspelling of "course."

coffin: The box in which a dead person's body is placed for burying,
crutch: A support which goes under the arm, used to help in walking,
disk: A flat circle-shaped plate,
dome: A cuplike cover to a building,
elevation: A raised place.

epileptic: A sufferer from epilepsy, a nervous disease.

excursion: A short journey, usually for pleasure.

exterior: On the outside. Being or occurring without.

extrodinarily: Susy's misspelling of "extraordinarily."

fathom: A unit of measurement equal to six feet, used in figuring the

depth of a river or other body of water.

fifty: Five times ten. Adjective — fiftieth.

fourteen: Four plus ten. Teen means to add ten to a number.

gingerbread: A light sweet cake flavored with ginger (a highly seasoned

flavoring) very popular in the U.S.

hymn: Song in praise or honor of God, a nation, etc.

interupt: Susy's misspelling of "interrupt."

invalid: One who is in bad health.

legislative: Law-making.

maried: Susy's misspelling of "married."

measles: An illness with fever and spots on the skin.

meningitis: A disease, especially affecting the brain.

mesmerism, -ist, -ize: Based on the theory of a man named Mesmer,

that one person can produce in another a condition like sleep in which

his mind is subject to the will of the operator.

minstrel: A singer of Negro tunes; a minstrel show was a favorite
entertainment where jokes were told, with one man acting as a sort of
director for the others.

Negro: A brown or black person of African blood.

phrenology: A system which believes in a relation between brains and

character and the formation of the structure of the head.

quack: One who pretends to medical skill; a false doctor.

royalty: A share based on a percentage of the earnings.

salon: A reception room in a large house.

superintendent: One who directs or manages.

surgery: The branch of medicine involving operations or instruments,
sute: Susy's misspelling of "suit."

syndicate: An association of people; in newspaper business, formed to

sell one story to a number of journals.

temperance: Not to drink alcohol or smoke tobacco, etc.

tenor: The highest adult male voice; a singer having such a voice,
tropics: Hot regions of the earth midway between the North and South
poles.

twain: old word for two.

villa: A house, particularly in Italy, with some suggestion of wealth,

vineyard: A place where grapes are grown,
ware: Susy's misspelling of "wear."

watermelon: A very large edible fruit with watery, sweet, red juice.

whisky: An alcoholic drink usually made from grain.

yacht: A ship specially built for pleasure (instead of war or commerce).

ILLUSTRATIONS

Printed by Amazon Italia Logistica S.r.l.
Torrazza Piemonte (TO), Italy